The publisher of *In Search of a Better Belief System,*
Ducks in a Row, and *The Man Who Lived Forever*
presents:

"Something like 8 out of every 10 people
just make up statistics on the spot!"

STOP
Pulling
Numbers
Out Of Your
ASS!

I0448020

8 out of 10
12 4
47%
the vast majority!"

What the actual FACTS reveal about life in America
...and the rest of the world!

Stop Pulling Numbers Out of Your Ass!
What the actual FACTS reveal about life in America and the
rest of the world!
© All rights reserved. I.M. Sharp

Paperback retail price: $9.95
ISBN-13: 978-1502717542
ISBN-10: 1502717549

Read more about *Pulling Numbers* & order the e-book
online at http://www.pullingnumbers.com

Published and distributed by
The Passion Profit Company
P.O. Box 618
Church Street Station
New York, NY 10008-0618
(646) 481-4238
www.PassionProfit.com
orderdept@passionprofit.com

TABLE OF CONTENTS

A THOUGHT: The blissification of America

"Do you smoke pot?" [US Marijuana use]
"SHE is probably a pot head!" [Marijuana use by age/race]
"The gays are gettin' married everywhere!" [Same sex by state]
"Some of my best friends are gay!" [Random same sex statistics]
"Mass shootings happen all the time!"[Mass murder]
"It was a killing spree!" [Mass murder another look]

A THOUGHT: Truth is a liberal idea

US POLITICS 35
"President Obama is a dictator!" [Presidential Executive Orders]
"The 'do nothing' Congress?" [Congressional bills]
"Did he/she really, actually say that???" [Quotes]
"Which millionaire should I vote for?" [Congressional net worth]
"Stop voter fraud!" [Voter fraud statistics]

A THOUGHT: Why America deserves Mitt Romney

EDUCATION 65
"Shouldn't you be in school right now?" [School attendance]
"How important are my SAT scores?" [SAT Statistics]
"I owe so much in loans!" [Student debt]
"Get an education to earn more money." [Education vs. salary]
"Why is an education so expensive" [Countries with free
education]

A THOUGHT:

The predictable progression of political pretense and prevarication

HEALTH & SURVIVAL 97

"This isn't the first ebola outbreak!" [Ebola outbreak history]

"Ebola is in the US!!!" [US ebola deaths]

"Too much sun is bad for you." [Health Myths]

"How to dodge a falling tree" [Counterintuitive Survival tips]

"You need chemo to treat cancer." [Cancer myth]

SPORTS & ENTERTAINMENT 105

"Sports salaries are out of control!" [Pro sports salaries]

"And he can't even act that well!" [Movie industry salaries]

"But, they don't make songs like they used to!"[Music Industry]

"Beatles? Stones? Michael Jackson? or Elvis?" [Best selling artist]

A THOUGHT: The fallacy of legality

SEX 111

"Why don't you wait until marriage?" [Pre-marital sex]

"Are you on the pill?" [Contraceptive use]

"Of course I watch porn, but..." [Porn consumption]

"Where is sex work legal?" [Sex work]

"He/she probably started at age 12!" [Sex work myths]

"She looks like a porn star!" [Porn industry]

A THOUGHT: Predictions

The dedication
This book is dedicated to my mother,
Thelma Rose Golding,
who helped me notice life's patterns

The acknowledgments
Ken McRae, Christine St. Hilaire, Reina Joa,
Ernest & Kim Capers, Tony Cordoza, Andrew Morrison,
Aaron & Stacey Spencer-Willoughby,
Nicole Drew, Kelly & Zelda Waters, Monica Afesi,
Diamond Davis, Carlton & Marian Gambrell,
Delxino & Deborah Wilson de Briano, Siew-Li Ng,
Chun Yu Wang, and Preeyaporn Promnoy Jompeang
for being part of my journey

Why?

"Something like 8 out of every 10 people
make up statistics on the spot."

❑ "Why did you write this book?" ❑

I often like to read the comments sections on articles on various news websites. There are always some gems to be discovered! Recently, in a long series of back and forth responses on one such site, between US Democrats and Republicans quoting all sorts of numbers and opinions to support each side's position on a recent article about former vice-presidential candidate, Paul Ryan, one fellow, adding his own take on all the dubious "facts" people were spewing, wrote:

"Something like 8 out of every 10 people make up statistics on the spot."

I thought that was hilarious!

Author, Rex Stout, famously said:

"There are two kinds of statistics, the kind you look up and the kind you make up."

It's so true. Whether it's about immigration, unemployment, welfare or war, there are statistics making the rounds through our media, at the water cooler, and around the family dinner table that are simply not true—the kind of statistics people are simply making up; numbers that people are—with apologies for the crudeness—simply pulling out of their asses! This book is my way of helping to address that sad reality!

How to tell when someone is pulling numbers out their ass

The next day, after stumbling upon that comment, I was listening to a podcast of the Jimmy Dore show in which an "economist" was asked to explain the income disparities between blacks and whites in America. He began spewing all sorts of racially charged stereotypes and buzzwords about unwed mothers being rewarded for having kids, the evils of a dependent culture, etc., and went on to say:

"..of course, the rates of birth out of wedlock, particularly in the black community, have gone up, I dunno, ten times in the past 50 years..."

"The vast majority, 80 or 90, er, I'm not sure of the figure exactly, of young black children are...."

That's a textbook case for your training for recognizing when someone is pulling numbers out of an ass: use of the phrases "I dunno," "something like," or "the vast majority," coupled with admitted lack of confidence and specificity when it comes to the actual numbers.

During the 2012 presidential campaign, Republican candidate, Rick Santorum, famously pulled numbers out his ass on numerous occasions (Google *"enforced euthanasia in the Netherlands"*), and most notably in classic style about the educational system in California:

SANTORUM: *"I was just reading something last night from the state of California. And that the California universities – I think it's seven or eight of the California system of universities, don't even teach an American history course. It's not even available to be taught."* Of course, Santorum's comments were later proven baseless.

Now, as you're aware, the concept of pulling numbers out of your own (or somebody else's) ass is not new. What's different now is that the practice, previously limited to (and forgivable) for those with limited access to information, now includes preachers, pundits, politicians, professors and even presidents! People in every walk of life are simply making up statistics to support their arguments....and it's driving the rest of us crazy!!!

Unlike in Rex Stout's day, people today don't even feel a need to look things up for verification. They start with bias, intolerance and prejudice as their platforms, and simply pull made up facts to support them! When you live in a country where no challenges the president of the United States when he tells obvious lies, then it sets a standard for its citizens to pull numbers out of their asses willy nilly…and believe they can get away with it!

If this book—while not the ultimate solution—can help in some small way to stop this insanity, then my efforts will not have been in vain!

These numbers have been checked and verified. Whip them out confidently at any dinner party to stop the madness!

Please remember, each page in this book represents a topic about which entire books have been written, years-long studies have been conducted and about which people have achieved professionally recognized expertise. My purpose in presenting these raw numbers and charts and summaries is simply to dispel some of the grosser misconceptions about certain basic and often-misrepresented topics and to help put other topics in perspective in a global context. It's important to note, however, that raw numbers can themselves be interpreted in many different ways. For instance, it's not enough to simply state that two countries have each incarcerated 50 people. If country "A" has a total population of 1,000 people, while country "B" has a total population of 51 people, then that same number of incarcerations (50) tells an entirely different story in each country. I've done my best to include additional information that helps provide a supplemental context and perspective to a bigger picture.

I've titled these topics in some provocative and politically incorrect ways just to give you some practice in recognizing the language that often indicates when a conversation is about to take a turn toward the rectum!

Every few pages, I'll also be sharing my observations in "thoughts" about various topics. These mini essays are my own opinions. Opinions?? In a book about facts??? Well, yes, I can do that, it's my book!

You'll get a refresher course in the basics, gain a new appreciation for how life in the US compares to the rest of the world, and at the very least, you'll discover some innovative and fascinating new sources of information* (See USdebtclock.org)!

With that said, let's begin our adventure, shall we? Join me, if you will, in a loud collective shout to those other folks to *"stop pulling numbers of your ass!"*

the "Source"info in the ebook/Kindle/Nook editions link directly to online source used. If you're reading the paperback edition, you're invited to search online using the source text.

A thought:
Everything you believe...is wrong!

This house of cards we refer to as our society's current belief system is crumbling. The cloak of deception

upon which that belief system is based is unraveling. Everything you've been told, believe and accept to be true about many aspects of reality is being challenged and exposed as simply false and wrong.

Priests are being exposed as predators. Politicians are being exposed as agenda-driven individualists rather than selfless public servants. Everything we believe is "progress" is unsustainable and is propelling our planet towards extinction. Everything you believe is "medicine" is often a set of untested drugs that unbalance the body's natural systems and cause more side effects than the illnesses they purport to cure.

Everything you believe is "food" is a concoction of chemically laden substances that are unusable by the body, deprive it of nutrients and its natural ability to heal.

Everything you believe is "economic growth through capitalism" is actually a money-grab that benefits only a select few at the expense of everyone else.

Everything you believe is "justice" is a punitive, revenge-focused, violence-based system of thought and action that support a prison industry designed to enrich its owners.

Everything you've been told are the "random" events of history might actually have been orchestrated.

Everything you believe to be "news" is opinion and, in many cases, completely contrived and staged.

Everything you're told to strive for in pursuit of success and freedom actually leads to failure and servitude.

Everything you've been told, and believe to be good, normal and necessary, desirable, ethical and moral are being revealed to be their exact opposites.

At the same time, everything you've been told and thus believe to be "evil sinful, impossible, absurd and abnormal" might actually be good, ethical, plausible, logical, quite normal and, in fact, in your best interest to explore, once truth is revealed.

The list goes on. Our beliefs about science, democracy, religion, government, education, the causes of war, the reasons behind assassinations, the existence of life on other planets, the origin of mankind, sexuality and various other concepts, ideas institutions and world views—all are being subjected to the onslaught of new questions and analyses and activism as people discover them to be other than what they've been led to believe.

They realize in many instances, that what they believe to be true is nothing more than a set of subjective ideas put forth by people who really don't have a handle on truth, don't know what they're doing, or worse, don't have your best interests at heart—people who are playing by a faulty rulebook or, worse, with no rule book at all.

Advertising = Education

Uninformed ideas, blind assumptions and outright lies underlie much of the education you received and advertising you are subjected to. In some instances, of course, education and advertising are one in the same. Take, for instance, the "education" you received in school about health and for instance the benefits of a meat-centered diet. These typically come from pamphlets created by a meat council—a conglomeration of meat producers—with a financial interest at stake (or at steak).

I'm sure you're familiar with many of these assumptions: that milk does a body good; that meat is real food for real people; that cancer can't be cured; that the common cold is inevitable; that allergies can only be relieved not ended; and that drugs these companies are pushing heal and aren't, in fact, more dangerous than the ills they claim to cure, given the extensive list of (sometimes fatal) side effects warned of in the disclaimers.

The sales pitches for these products start with these assumptions and are never challenged. As a result, people buy into them (key word "buy"), and continue a vicious cycle perpetuating the very lifestyle that caused their ills.

The end result: Why all this matters
"Every day, people are attempting to influence your purchases, sway your allegiance, stoke your emotions and win your vote, using numbers and "facts" that are simply not true. Without the correct information, you will be their victim."

Why is this important? Well, without the correct paradigm for your body and how it operates, you will find that health eludes you despite your best efforts at eating healthy and living a healthy lifestyle. Without the correct paradigm for health and how to achieve it, you will find that as you "cure" one ailment you create another.

If I believed, for example, that "milk does a body good," and then acted on that belief (by drinking lots of milk) in an effort to improve my health, I might find myself experiencing colds, mucous, allergies, weakened bones and cancer, and eventually become frustrated in my efforts without ever knowing the real reason why: that the dairy products we've been told are beneficial, are, in fact poison to our systems (and the numbers prove it)!

Without the correct numbers, you will compromise your health, your safety, make generally poor decisions and put yourself and others at risk and in harm's way. Think of *Stop Pulling Numbers Out of Your Ass* as a course in survival. When it comes to survival, you cannot rely on numbers pulled out an ass! Let's begin!

Life In America

"Americans live not by facts, but by a lengthy list of myths." — **Dave Champion**

"We live in a world where unfortunately the distinction between true and false appears to become increasingly blurred by manipulation of facts, by exploitation of uncritical minds, and by the pollution of the language." — **Arne Tiselius**

"I'm tired of ignorance held up as inspiration, where vicious anti-intellectualism is considered a positive trait, and where uninformed opinion is displayed as fact." — **Phil Plait**

"All opinions are not equal. Some are a very great deal more robust, sophisticated and well supported in logic and argument than others." — **Doug Adams**, *The Salmon of Doubt*

1. ❑ "How many of us/them are there?" ❑

[US population by race]

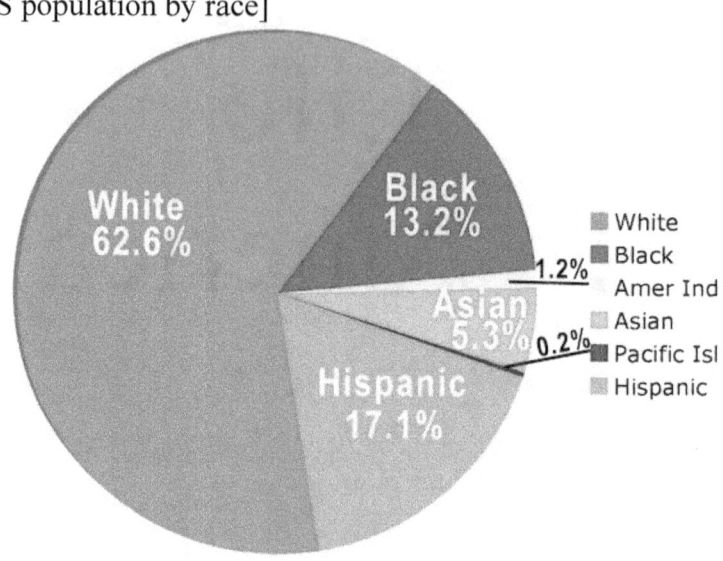

Population, 2014 estimate	319,283,128
White alone, percent 2013 (a)	77.7%
Black or African American alone percent 2013	13.2%
American Indian Alaska Native alone 2013	1.2%
Asian alone, percent 2013, (a)	5.3%
Native Hawaiian/Pacific Islander alone 2013	0.2%
Mixed Races percent 2013	2.4%
Hispanic or Latino percent 2013 (b)	17.1%
White alone not Hispanic or Latino 2013	62.6%
Veterans 2008-2012	21,853,912
Households 2008-2012	115,226,802
Persons per household, 2008-2012	2.61
Money income in past year (2012 dollars)	$28,051
Median household income, 2008-2012	$53,046
Persons below poverty level, 2008-2012	14.9%
Persons per square mile, 2010	87.4

Source: US Census Quick Facts (adjusted for 2013)

2. ❑ "Actually, I know a lot about America!" ❑

[US general knowledge] Here are some numbers:

Birth and beyond:
Birth rate: 13.42 births/1,000 population (2014 est.)
Death rate: 8.15 deaths/1,000 population (2014 est.)
Life expectancy at birth: total population: 79.56 years
Life expectancy male: 77.11 years
Life expectancy female: 81.94 years (2014 est.)

Debt:

The national debt:	17 Trillion +
Debt per US citizen:	$56,172
Debt per taxpayer:	$153,268

Literacy:

Literacy rate:	99%

Employment:

Current unemployment rate:	5.8% (Oct 2014)
Self-employed:	8.95 million
"Officially" unemployed	8,914,940
Actual unemployed	17,852,097
Food Stamp recipients:	46,243,541

Size
Land area in square miles, 2010:   3,531,905.43
about half the size of Russia; about three-tenths the size of Africa; about half the size of South America (or slightly larger than Brazil); slightly larger than China; more than twice the size of the European Union

Sources: Bureau of Labor Statistics, USDebtClock.org CIA.gov

3. ❑ "There are too many immigrants!" ❑

[Legal resident info] The myth: Immigration is out of control!

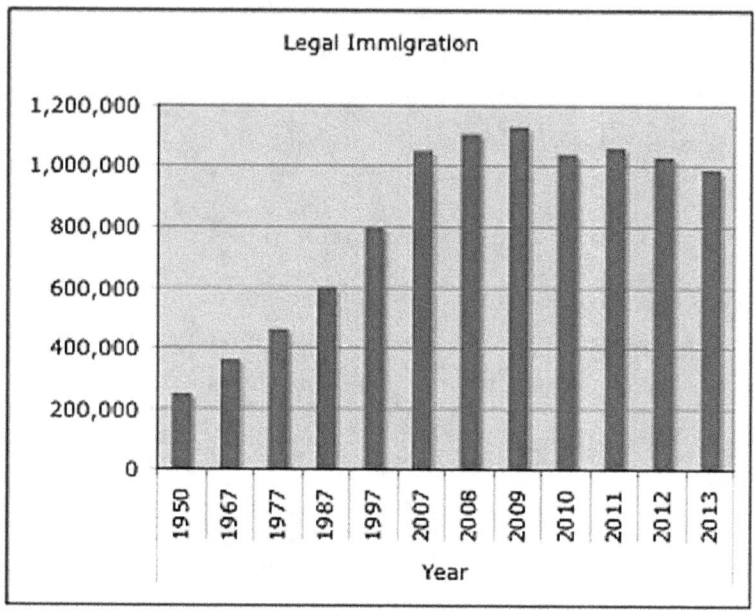

The number of <u>legal</u> immigrants to the US has been declining from a high during 2009. These are individuals who have obtained their permanent resident ("green card") status each year.

2009 : 1,130,818
2010 : 1,042,625
2011 : 1,062,040
2012 : 1,031,631
2013 :   990,553

Source: US Department of Homeland Security, *Persons Obtaining Legal Permanent Resident Status: Fiscal Years 1950 to 2013*

4. ❏ "Where do new citizens come from?" ❏

[New citizens by country]

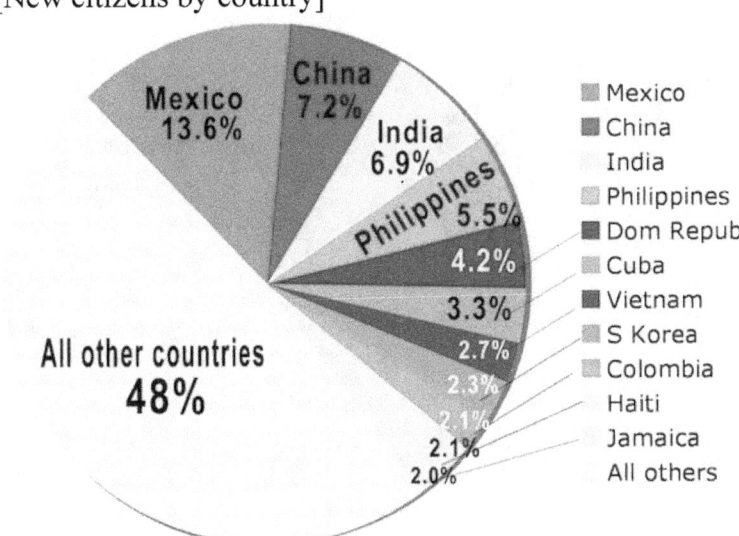

Actual numbers:
Total: 990,553

Mexico	135,028	Jamaica	19,400
China	71,798	El Salvador	18,260
India	68,458	Nigeria	13,840
Philippines	54,446	Pakistan	13,251
Dom Repub	41,311	Canada	13,181
Cuba	32,219	Ethiopia	13,097
Vietnam	27,101	Nepal	13,046
S Korea	23,166	UK	12,984
Colombia	21,131	Iran	12,863
Haiti	20,351	Burma	12,565
		All others	353,057

Source: Department of Homeland Security (2013 numbers)

5. ❑ "Send 'em back where they came from!"❑

[Illegal immigration] By definition, of course, illegal immigration defies measurement. However, for 2012, the Department of Homeland Security estimates that there are 11.4 million unauthorized immigrants living in the United States, down from 11.5 million in 2011. The top countries of origin are: Mexico (59%), El Salvador (6%), Guatemala (5%), Honduras (3%), Philippines (3%)

2012 - The top U.S. states where unauthorized immigrants settle are: California (25%), Texas (16%), Florida (6%), New York (5%), Illinois (5%)

Unauthorized immigrants to the United States tend to be young (61% between ages 25-44) and male (53%). However, 57% of unauthorized immigrants over the age of 45 are female.

In 2012, figures show 643,474 unauthorized immigrants are apprehended.

There are approximately 8 million illegal aliens in the US workforce.

Unaccompanied Alien Children (UAC):
     FY2014 - 60,000 (estimate)
     FY2013 - 24,668
     FY2012 - 14,721

Sources: DHS, CNN, US Customs & Border Protection

6. ❏ "Why aren't we deporting them?"❏

[Deportation]   Are   deportations   increasing   or decreasing?

Figure 1. Deportations: 1982 - 2011

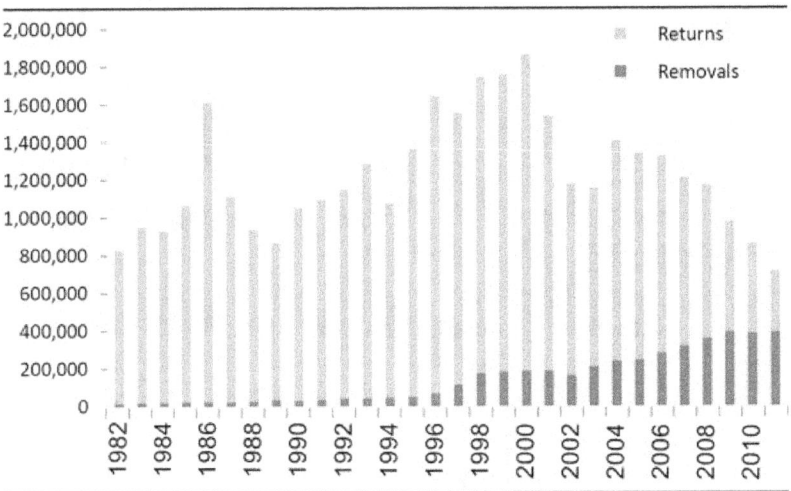

Source: DHS

Total deportations peaked in 2000 and has been declining. However, the total number of *removals* (a subset of total deportations) has been increasing.

A *return* is *"the confirmed movement of an inadmissible or deportable alien out of the United States not based on an order of removal"* (formerly "voluntary departure).

A *removal* is *"the compulsory and confirmed movement of an inadmissible or deportable alien out of the United States based on an order of removal.* It is a harsher consequence than a return, because it bars the deportee from re-entry for a certain number of years and carries the potential for prison time if the deportee re-enters illegally.

Less people are being deported, but the manner in which they are being deported is increasingly more severe.

Source: *Department of Homeland Security*

7. ❑ "Everyone wants to be American!" ❑

[Renouncing US citizenship] Almost 3,000 Americans renounced their citizenship in 2013*. The 2010 passage of FATCA (Foreign Accounts Tax Compliance Act) requiring foreign banks to report information on US deposit holders is a major contributor to recent increases. Most countries don't tax their citizens living abroad. For example, a German living in Switzerland won't pay German taxes, only Swiss taxes. The U.S. taxes its citizens wherever they are in the world. The only other country that does this is Eritrea.

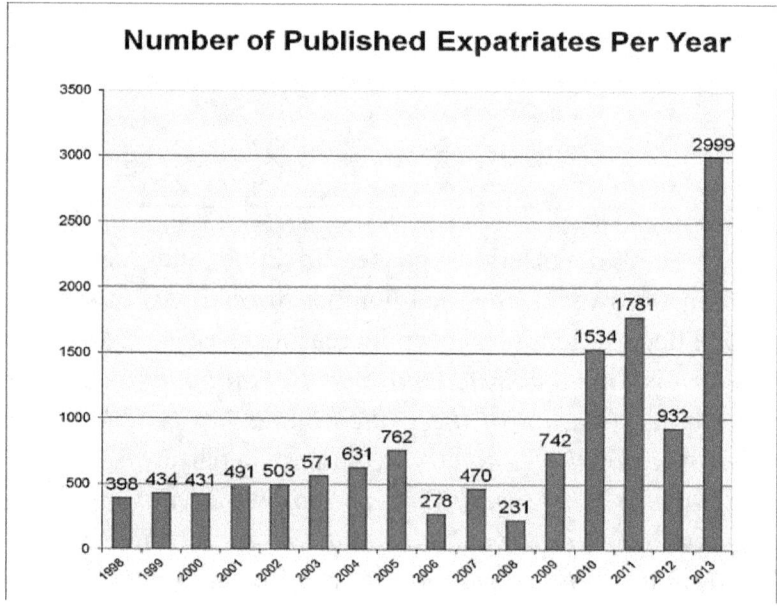

*At least one organization (The Isaac Brock Society) alleges that the Federal Register's list (a.k.a. the "name and shame" list) does not include certain high profile individuals who are known to have renounced in 2013 and that actual figures may be as high as 50,000 each year.

Sources: US Treasury Department via International Tax Blog; Federal Register; Isaac Brock Society

A thought:
The nature of lies

Let's explore a few thoughts about lies and deception, for this will serve us well in any discussion where someone is pulling numbers out of his/her ass. Let's start by broadening our understanding.

There are two types of lies: lies of commission and lies of omission; things that are done, and things that are not done; things said, and things left unsaid.

Anything that omits the truth is a lie.

Anything that distorts the truth is a lie.

Anything that reduces truth is a lie.

Anything that is intended to replace truth is a lie.

Anything that delays revelation of truth is a lie.

It's been said that the only way to control someone is to lie to them. There is always some sort of agenda behind lies. The motivation that typically underlies (pun intended) the omission, distortion, reduction, replacement and delay of fact are one or more of the following: survival, power and wealth. An activist lies to create a cause for which she can get funding to survive. A politician lies to create a common "enemy" (the other side, welfare recipients, etc.) to galvanize public sentiment to get votes, to put himself in a position of power from which he creates wealth for himself. A war profiteer lies to create the justification for war, through which he can get military contracts. Such is the nature of lies.

8. ❑ "HE is probably on welfare!" ❑

[Welfare stats by race] Temporary Assistance for Needy Families is a US federal assistance program. It began on July 1, 1996, and succeeded the Aid to Families with Dependent Children (AFDC) program, providing cash assistance to indigent American families with dependent children through the United States Department of Health and Human Services. This cash benefit is often referred to simply as "welfare."

Trend in TANF Families by Race/Ethnicity 2000 - 2010

	All Open cases	White	Black or Af Amer	Latin	Nativ Amer	Asian
2000	2,269,131	31.2%	38.6%	25.0%	1.6%	2.2%
2001	1,408,752	32.2%	39.0%	23.6%	1.3%	2.5%
2002	1,315,029	34.2%	38.9%	21.6%	1.6%	2.2%
2003	1,248,570	35.1%	38.6%	20.5%	1.7%	2.0%
2004	1,168,539	36.7%	38.9%	19.1%	1.7%	1.5%
2005	1,092,018	36.3%	38.3%	19.8%	1.6%	1.9%
2006	996,312	37.9%	37.2%	19.9%	1.5%	1.7%
2007	941,040	35.9%	36.4%	22.6%	1.4%	2.0%
2008	869,463	35.2%	35.0%	23.3%	1.5%	2.6%
2009	973,580	35.4%	34.1%	24.2%	1.4%	2.3%
2010	1,084,828	36.8%	33.0%	23.7%	1.2%	2.4%
2011	1,104,266	34.5%	34.7%	24.2%	1.2%	2.4%
2012	1,009,349	34.0%	33.5%	25.7%	1.2%	2.4%

The number of whites on welfare is the highest it's been since 2000. The number of blacks on welfare has been decreasing and is less as of 2012 than it was in 2000.

Source: US Department of Health & Human Services "Characteristics and Financial Circumstances of TANF Recipients" by fiscal year

9. ❑ "Those @#$%^& minimum wage workers!"❑

[Stats for minimum wage workers]

Last year 1.532 million hourly workers earned the federal minimum of $7.25 an hour; nearly 1.8 million more earned less than that because they fell under one of several exemptions (tipped employees, full-time students, certain disabled workers and others), for a total of 3.3 million hourly workers at or below the federal minimum.

People at or below federal minimum are mostly:
Young: 50.4% are ages 16 to 24;
Teen: 24% are teenagers (16 to 19).
White (77%);
Women (nearly half are white women)
Largely part-time workers (64% of total)

2013 Figures:

OCCUPATIONAL GROUP	WORKFORCE
Food preparation and serving related occupations	1,540,000
Sales and related occupations	477,000
Personal care and service occupations	228,000
Office and administrative support occupations	196,000
Building and grounds cleaning and maintenance occupations	183,000
Transportation and material moving occupations	171,000
Professional and related occupations	119,000
Production occupations	105,000
Healthcare support occupations	87,000
Protective service occupations	61,000
Management, business, and financial operations occupations	38,000
Construction and extraction occupations	38,000
Farming, fishing and forestry occupations	35,000
Installation, maintenance and repair occupations	21,000

Source: Bureau of Labor Statistics via Pew Research

10. ☐ "The unemployment rate is going up!" ☐
[Unemployment rate]

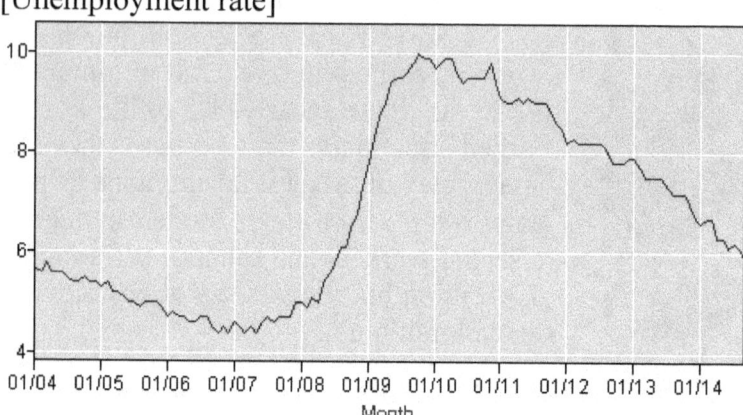

January of each year since 2004; 16 years old and over

Year	Jan	Feb	Mar	Apr	May	Jun	Jul	Aug	Sep	Oct	Nov	Dec	Annual
2004	5.7	5.6	5.8	5.6	5.6	5.6	5.5	5.4	5.4	5.5	5.4	5.4	
2005	5.3	5.4	5.2	5.2	5.1	5.0	5.0	4.9	5.0	5.0	5.0	4.9	
2006	4.7	4.8	4.7	4.7	4.6	4.6	4.7	4.7	4.5	4.4	4.5	4.4	
2007	4.6	4.5	4.4	4.5	4.4	4.6	4.7	4.6	4.7	4.7	4.7	5.0	
2008	5.0	4.9	5.1	5.0	5.4	5.6	5.8	6.1	6.1	6.5	6.8	7.3	
2009	7.8	8.3	8.7	9.0	9.4	9.5	9.5	9.6	9.8	10.0	9.9	9.9	
2010	9.7	9.8	9.9	9.9	9.6	9.4	9.5	9.5	9.5	9.5	9.8	9.4	
2011	9.1	9.0	9.0	9.1	9.0	9.1	9.0	9.0	9.0	8.8	8.6	8.5	
2012	8.2	8.3	8.2	8.2	8.2	8.2	8.2	8.1	7.8	7.8	7.8	7.9	
2013	7.9	7.7	7.5	7.5	7.5	7.5	7.3	7.2	7.2	7.2	7.0	6.7	
2014	6.6	6.7	6.7	6.3	6.3	6.1	6.2	6.1	5.9	5.8			

Chart shows unemployment rate for those 16 years and older, for each month of the year from 2004 to the date of publication of this book.

Source: Bureau of Labor Statistics dynamic chart

11. ❏ "SHE is probably unemployed!" ❏
[Unemployment rate by race]

Percent

Shaded areas represent recessions as determined by the National Bureau of Economic Research (NBER). Persons of Hispanic or Latino ethnicity may be of any race. Data for Asians (not seasonally adjusted) are not available before 2000.

Source: Bureau of Labor Statistics, Current Pop Survey, Oct 3, 2014

12. ❑ "I wonder how much they make?"❑

[Random salaries] Ever wanted to compare what certain professions or personalities earn as a salary? Here is a random list arranged from lowest to highest.

Profession/Position	Per hour	Avg Annual Salary	High and Low
Mcdonald's crewmem	$8.09	-	$7 to $11/hr
Fast food cook	$9.08	$18,870	
Walmart associate	$9.23		$7 to $18/hr
Farmworkers	$9.65	$20,080	
Amusemnt park atten	$9.76	$20,310	
Childcare worker	$10.33	$21,490	
Slaughterhouse	$12.21	$25,400	
Garbage collector	$16.96	$35,280	$18k to $58k
McDonald's manager	-	$43,095	$27 to $57
Flight attendant	-	$43,860	
Correctional officer	$21.26	$44,350	
Walmart Asst managr	-	$46,734	$36k to $70k
High School Teacher	-	$55,050	
Electrical Engineer	$44.89	$93,380	
Veterinarian	$46.22	$96,140	
Dentist	$81.19	$168,870	
Surgeon	$112.09	$233,150	
Phil Jackson Knicks	-	$12 million	
CEO Goldman Sachs	-	$19.9 million	
CEO Coca Cola		$20.3 million	
Kobe Bryant		$30.4 million	
CEO CBS Corp		$66.9 million	
CEO Cheniere Energ		$141.9 million	

Note: these are straight salaries and do not include bonuses, profit sharing, residuals, royalties, etc.

Sources: Bureau of Labor Statistics, Glassdoor, AFLCIO, ESPN

A thought:
The Standard American Racial Skew (SARS)

Even "raw" data and observation can be biased

Many years ago in college, I took an anthropology course. On the first day of class, the professor challenged us to describe a normal, everyday scene from the perspective of an alien visiting from another planet. For instance, imagine that you had to describe your morning routine (shower, shave, exercise, breakfast) from the perspective of someone who has never lived on the planet Earth. As each student shared his/her account, the professor showed us just how much of our "observations" as well as the language we used to describe them were actually based on experience, knowledge, interpretation that were all culturally-specific. (Tip: if you use words like "soap," "clean," "wash," "food," and "eat" you're using earth-centric concepts that have no meaning outside of our galaxy.) That exercise served me well for all my life to be able to see things objectively with less of a cultural bias.

The point is that without such training or practice, people tend to see others the way they see themselves. People tend to ascribe to others the same motivations, fears, and worldview they themselves have and are typically oblivious to how culturally biased they may be.

The Standard American Racial Skew (SARS)

Here in America, the white supremacist bias influences everything from dating advice, travel tips, even medical diagnoses and "skin toned" Band-Aids. All are based on a white person's experience and worldview. Authors, researchers, marketers and even scientists are often simply unaware that alternate worldviews, cultural norms, and even physiologies exist, and extrapolate a US white (typically male) model as being representative of the population at large.

Despite what you have been led to believe, we are all the same in how we see the world, how we see ourselves and even what we want from life. Even polling (i.e. who is polled, what they are asked, and how they respond) must often be customized, interpreted and filtered for different racial, ethnic, cultural and religious groups. A dating/relationship advice book based on the experience of a white male living in Harlem is not applicable to a black male living in Japan. Both men and women in each country are raised with different gender roles, cultural expectations.

A perfect example of this can be seen and studied in the 2008 and 2012 US presidential elections in which the Republican-leaning pollsters and pundits (white males polling white males and white communities, and speaking from a white male worldview), were so far out of touch with the ethnic and worldview realities of the voting public that they missed the Obama landslide victory that ensued....twice! They were victims of SARS, the Standard American Racial Skew characterized by a blatant disregard for others' reality. As the color of the nation changes, the ability of such pundits and pollsters and predictors to see "beyond the pale," will become increasingly valuable.

The War Monger Disposition (WMD)

This type of tunnel vision is not only racial and cultural in nature. There is also what I call the warmonger disposition (WMD) that you'll see evidenced everywhere in our society. There is a language of war that permeates the culture. When interviewing for a job, your skill set becomes an arsenal. Even relationships become adversarial engagements where one side has to win in a "battle of the sexes." We trivialize, glorify and jade ourselves to the horrors of killing other human beings when we, the media (and even our president) refer to murder, executions and assassinations of enemy combatants as "taking him out."

We wage a "war against ebola" instead of healing those suffering from the virus. We wage a "war on drugs" instead of eliminating the root cause of addictions. We "kill" two birds with one stone, and the list goes on.

Having a hard time finding other words we could use? Well, consider if, instead of fighting and battling, we were to "heal," "treat," "fix," or "cure" problems instead?

SARS and WMD are just two of many paradigms that often interfere with our objectivity as we seek to interpret the numbers in the world that includes females, homosexuals and all stripes of ethnic diversity!

13. ❑ "Do you support the death penalty?" ❑

[Death Penalty] Support for the death penalty has been declining over the past 18 years. Since 1996, the margin between those who favor the death penalty and those who oppose it has narrowed from a 60-point gap (78% favor vs. 18% oppose) in 1996 to an 18-point difference in 2013 (55% favor vs. 37% oppose).

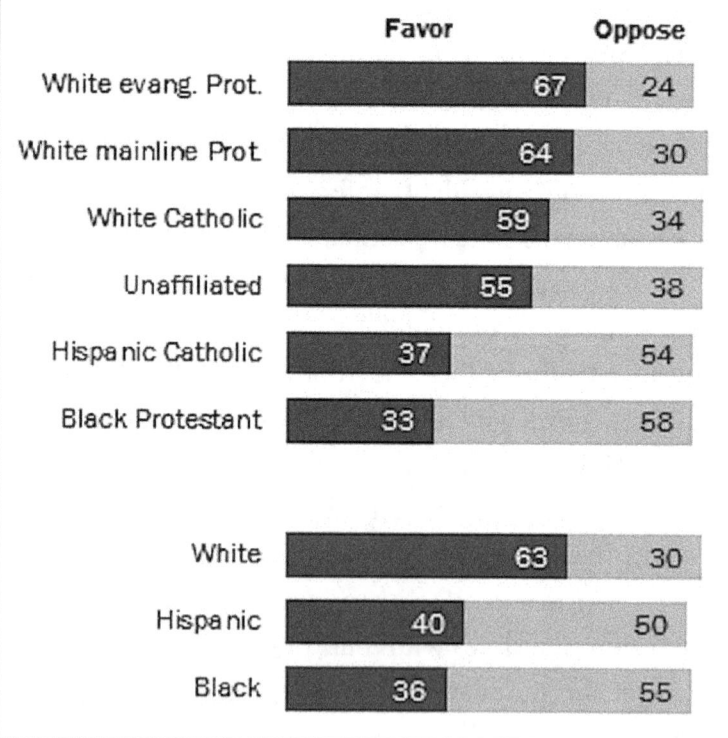

Support for Death Penalty Across Religious and Racial/Ethnic Groups

% of U.S. adults who favor/oppose the death penalty for those convicted of murder

	Favor	Oppose
White evang. Prot.	67	24
White mainline Prot.	64	30
White Catholic	59	34
Unaffiliated	55	38
Hispanic Catholic	37	54
Black Protestant	33	58
White	63	30
Hispanic	40	50
Black	36	55

Source: Pew Research March/April 2013

14. ❑ "Who did we execute in 2014?" ❑

[Death penalty executions by age, race, victim]

Date	ST	Name of executed	Age	Race	Victim	*
1/7/14	FL	Askari Muhammad	62	B	White	30
1/9/14	OK	Michael Wilson	38	B	White	16
1/16/14	OH	Dennis McGuire	53	W	White	20
1/22/14	TX	Edgar Tamayo~	46	L	White	20
1/24/14	OK	Kenneth Hogan	52	W	White	11
1/29/14	MO	Herbert Smulls	56	B	White	22
2/5/14	TX	Suzanne Basso*f*	59	W	White	15
2/12/14	FL	Juan Chavez~	46	L	White	16
2/26/14	MO	Michael Taylor	47	B	White	23
2/26/14	FL	Paul Howell	48	B	White	9
3/19/14	TX	Ray Jasper	33	B	Latino	14
3/20/14	FL	Robert Henry	55	B	1W, 1B	26
3/26/14	MO	Jeffrey Ferguson	59	W	White	19
3/27/14	TX	Anthony Doyle	29	B	Asian	10
4/3/14	TX	Tommy Sells	49	W	White	14
4/9/14	TX	Ramiro Hernandez~	44	L	White	14
4/16/14	TX	Jose Villegas	39	L	Latino	12
4/23/14	MO	William Rousan	57	W	White	18
4/23/14	FL	Robert Hendrix	47	W	White	23
4/29/14	OK	Clayton Lockett	38	B	White	14
6/17/14	GA	Marcus Wellons	58	B	Black	21
6/18/14	MO	John Winfield	46	B	Black	16
6/18/14	FL	John Henry	63	B	White	23
7/10/14	FL	Eddie Davis	45	W	White	19
7/16/14	MO	John Middleton	54	W	White	17
7/23/14	AZ	Joseph Wood	55	W	White	23
8/6/14	MO	M. Worthington	43	W	White	16
9/10/14	MO	Earl Ringo Jr.	40	B	White	16
9/10/14	TX	Willie Trottie	45	B	Black	21
9/17/14	TX	Lisa Coleman *f*	38	B	Black	8
10/28/14	TX	Miguel Paredes	32	L	1 L,1W	14

*Years from sentencing to execution. All by lethal injection.
f =female   ~ =foreign national
¥ = white defendant for murder of black victim
Source: Death Penalty Information Center

15. ❏ "There aren't enough people in jail!" ❏
[Incarceration statistics]

	2011		2012	
Total	6,978,500	100%	6,937,600	100%
Probation	3,971,300	56.9%	3,942,800	56.8%
Parole	853,900	12.2%	851,200	12.3%
Prison	1,505,000	21.6%	1,483,900	21.4%
Local jail	735,600	10.5%	744,500	10.7%
*Offenders	87,200	00%	84,700	00%

About 6,937,600 offenders were under the supervision of adult correctional systems at yearend 2012, declining by about 51,000 offenders during the year.

The decrease during 2012 was the fourth consecutive year of decline in the correctional population.

In 2012 about 1 in every 35 adults in the US, or 2.9% of adult residents, was on probation or parole or incarcerated in prison or jail, the same rate as in 1997.

An estimated 1 in every 50 adult residents was supervised in the community on probation or parole at yearend 2012, compared to 1 in every 108 adults incarcerated in prison or jail.

Probation: supervision in the community through a probation agency, generally in lieu of incarceration.
Parole: conditional release from prison to serve the remaining portion of a sentence in the community.
Jails are locally operated, short-term facilities that hold inmates awaiting trial or sentencing, and inmates sentenced to a term of less than 1 year, typically misdemeanants. *Prisons* are long term facilities run by the state or federal government and typically hold felons and inmates with sentences of more than 1 year.

Source: Correctional Populations in the United States, 2012

16. ☐ "I said there aren't enough people in jail!" ☐

[Incarceration trends] There are many ways to parse and present incarceration statistics: by gender, by race, by age, etc. However, of most compelling significance is simply the trend of increasing numbers since 1978.

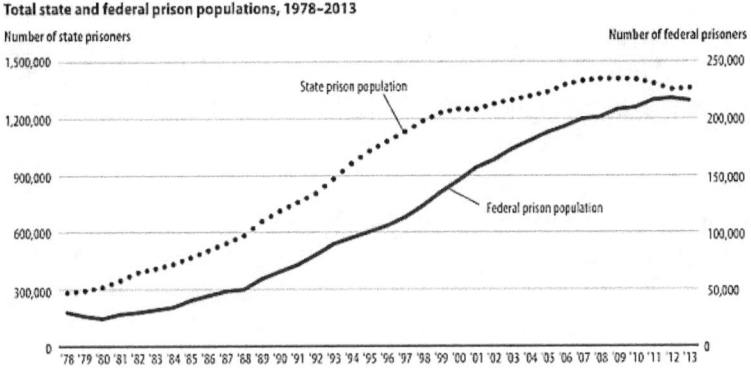

Total state and federal prison populations, 1978-2013

Note: Counts based on all prisoners under the jurisdiction of state and federal correctional authorities.

On Dec 31, 2013, the US held an estimated 1,574,700 persons in state and federal prisons, an increase of approximately 4,300 (0.3%) from 2012. This was the first increase since the peak of 1,615,500 in 2009. These figures do not include those on probation or parole.

Source: Department of Justice, Bureau of Justice Statistics
"Prisoners in 2013" E. Ann Carson, Ph.D., BJS Statistician

17. ☐ "HE is probably a felon!" ☐

[Prison population by race]

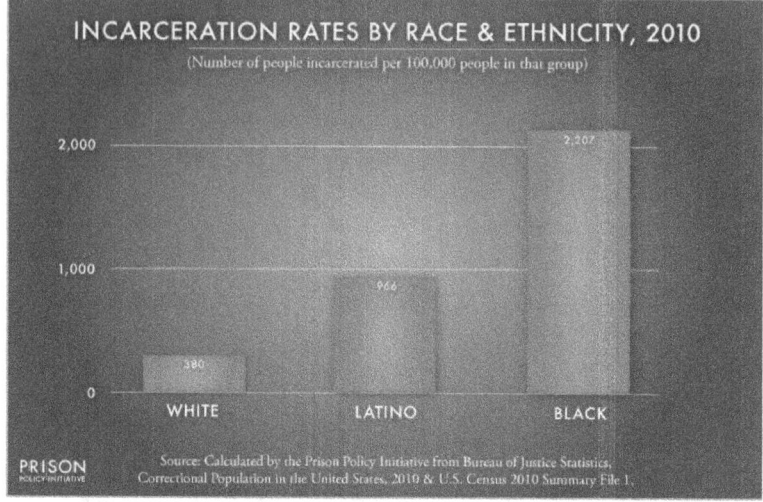

Number of prisoners per 100,000 in each group

Race/Ethnicity	% of US population	% of U.S. incarcerated population	National incarceration rate (per 100,000)
White (non-Hispanic)	64%	39%	450 per 100,000
Hispanic	16%	19%	831 per 100,000
Black	13%	40%	2,306 per 100,000

Compared to overall population.

The reason these figures cause concern is that one would expect the percentages in *prison* population to reflect the percentages in the *general* US population. However, according to the U.S. Census, Blacks are incarcerated five times more than Whites. Furthermore, Hispanics are nearly twice as likely to be incarcerated as Whites. Stated a different way: almost 3% of all black male U.S. residents of all ages were imprisoned on December 31, 2013, compared to 0.5% of white males.

Sources: Prison Policy Initiative; Bureau of Prisons

18. ❑ "And just so we're clear:" ❑

It is clear by now to observers outside the US as well as those within that who is being imprisoned and who is committing crimes are two almost unrelated statistics. In a historically, institutionally and profoundly racist society like the US, there is a tendency to stop and frisk that is racially biased, a tendency to arrest and initiate a criminal record that is racially biased, a tendency to prosecute that is racially biased, a tendency to convict that is racially biased, as well as racial disparities in sentencing for the same crimes, and a tendency to kill prisoners (i.e. the death penalty) that is racially biased. Therefore, one cannot simply look at arrest, prosecution, conviction, incarceration or death penalty numbers to determine who is committing the crimes.

"I don't even talk about whether or not racial profiling is legal. I just don't think racial profiling is a particularly good law enforcement tool."--Eric Holder, Attorney General of the United States.

19. ❑ "Get off your ass and get a job!" ❑

[Poverty & Homelessness in America] 31 states saw a decrease in homelessness, while 20 states saw increases in overall homelessness.

The national rate of homelessness fell to 19 homeless persons per 10,000 people in the general population, but the rate in individual states ranged from 106 in Washington, DC to 8 in Mississippi.

The rate of veteran homelessness fell to 27 homeless veterans per 10,000 veterans in the general population, but the rate in individual states ranged from 28 in Wyoming to 156 in Wash.DC.

Nationally, the number of people in poverty increased slightly, by 0.6 percent with 24 states experiencing an increase.

The poverty rate remained unchanged at 15.9 percent, but the rate in individual states ranged from 10 percent in New Hampshire to 24 percent in Mississippi.

Unemployment decreased 9.6 percent nationally and in all but four states from 2011 to 2012 and the unemployment rate ranged state by state from 3 percent in North Dakota to 11 percent in Nevada.

The number of poor rental households experiencing severe housing cost burden, meaning households in poverty paying more than 50 percent of their income toward housing, increased slightly nationally, by 0.7 percent. Yet, 25 states still saw decreases.

The number of people in poor households living doubled up with family/friends remained relatively stable nationally, decreasing in 27 states and increasing in 24.

Source: National Alliance to End Homelessness

A thought:
The "blissification" of America

Ignorance = intelligence

Something very sinister is happening in America: ignorance is being put on equal footing as intelligence. I call it the "ignorance is blissificiation of America" where:

(a) so-called pundits are given national stages for their outlandish opinions, blatant biases and pernicious prejudices and are thus legitimized in public opinion.

(b) logic, critical analysis and fact checking are considered evil and subversive.

(c) idiots are allowed to run for the highest elected office.

Consequently, the bar of competence has been lowered, and the next generation believes their personal views—no matter how ill-informed, societally-abhorrent or destructive—must, as a matter of course, be taken seriously, and that they are deserving of (no, entitled to), a platform for their views simply by virtue of having them.

You may call this the beauty of democracy—where even the least among us can rise to the top. However, giving equal time to idiots creates a society where higher education, basic reasoning and analytical skills, simple geography knowledge, spelling, grammar and enunciation are viewed as snobbish. No good can come of this.

Opinion = fact

If this weren't bad enough, the public is being led to believe debates exist where none actually do.

"Global Warming? What's your opinion?" Despite what you've been led to believe, the science is not "out" on this. We are beyond debate here. We have construed "every one is equal" to mean everyone's opinion should be given equal merit on the same stage. People think that freedom of speech means (a) freedom to hold any viewpoint—however biased and outlandish, and (b) that said viewpoint must be given equal merit simply because it can be stated in words. That's insanity!

You can find evidence of this in news reporting. Essentially, news today is reported as if truth and facts don't exist. There are no investigations. There is no stand for what is true and provable. Every issue is portrayed as two-sided with equal weight on each side. Particularly on issues that can be skewed to be "Republican vs. Democrat" or "liberal vs. conservative," we are encouraged to think that the truth is some unknowable and mysterious thing that exists somewhere in the middle of the two sides and that we might someday be able to uncover the truth given the right tools. Global warming, voter fraud, the truth of Ebola transmission, are essentially all being presented as two-sided like this:

"The Cubs played the Dodgers last night. The Cubs said they won. The Dodgers said they won. I guess we'll never know the answer. This is John Smith reporting for Faux News." (credit: comedian, Jimmy Dore, for baseball metaphor)

Your ideas = your politics

In the faux debate that ensues from such insanity, certain ideas have been tagged as partisan. The idea that one can rely on evidence and research to prove a point is now considered "liberal" and left wing, while all things religious and faith-based are tagged as "conservative."

We lower the bar of discourse

Listen to politicians being interviewed or debated and you'll notice that questions are answered with evasive non-answers, platforms are reduced to mere talking points, and emotionally charged platitudes are used to hijack intellectual discussions. Candidates for office misspeak, misrepresent and mispronounce. The bar for educated discourse of the society's ills has been lowered.

We put the sociopaths in charge

sociopath. *n. a person with a personality disorder manifesting itself in extreme antisocial attitudes and behavior and a lack of conscience.*

It stands to reason and logic that certain jobs attract certain personality types. "Caretakers" become doctors and nurses. "Gurus" become teachers and instructors. Politics, by its very nature tends to attract power-hungry sociopaths.

Don't believe me? Here are ten telltale signs of the sociopathic personality.

1) Sociopaths are charming. Sociopaths have high charisma and tend to attract a following just because people want to be around them.

2) Sociopaths are more spontaneous and intense

3) Sociopaths are incapable of feeling shame, guilt or remorse. They pursue any action that serves their own self-interest even if it seriously harms others. This is why you will find many very "successful" sociopaths in high levels of government, in any nation.

4) Sociopaths invent outrageous lies about their experiences. They wildly exaggerate things to the point of absurdity, but when they describe it to you in a storytelling format, for some reason it sounds believable at the time.

5) Sociopaths seek to dominate and "win" at all costs.

6) Sociopaths tend to be highly intelligent, but they use their brainpower to deceive others rather than empower

7) Sociopaths are incapable of love

8) Sociopaths are master wordsmiths.

9) Sociopaths never apologize. They are never wrong. They never feel guilt. They can never apologize. Even if shown proof that they were wrong, they will refuse to apologize and instead go on the attack.

10) Sociopaths are delusional and literally believe that what they say becomes truth.

(Source: The Sociopath Next Door, via NaturalNews.com)

Did any politicians come to mind when you were reading that list? (Mitt Romney? Bill Clinton? Paul Ryan? Rand Paul?) Of course, we as a society aren't eager to admit that the people we are electing to public office are, in fact, sociopaths, but the evidence is there and it's clear.

It is a very scary prospect to realize that the entire political system has been based on electing to public office individuals who by the very fact and act of their pursuit of such power disqualifies them as qualified candidates. In other words, as I always say, *the very last person we should elect to a position of power is the individual who seeks it.*

Our entire electoral process is an elaborate construct designed/evolved to weed *in* the richer, more driven, more sociopathic, less empathetic, more devious, self-centered candidates without a moral compass, while weeding *out* the poorer, more morally guided individuals.

More tragic, is that people continue to elect, and then hold these elected individuals to the same standards of decency and morality when they are functionally incapable of it. These are not normal people. These are not rational people. These are not people for whom evidence has any meaning. We know this because when confronted with evidence of the latest transgression and scandal, they continue to maintain their positions, or (a) change their position and maintain the evidence is not real, (b) attack the messenger, (c) claim they were misquoted, or (d) all of the above. This is sociopathic behavior.

You cannot use logic to appeal to a sociopath to change his ways, nor can you use evidence to force him to admit his errors. It's a battle that cannot be won. As eloquently stated by author, Sam Harris:

"If someone doesn't value evidence, what evidence are you going to provide to prove that they should value it?

If someone doesn't value logic, what logical argument could you provide to show the importance of logic?"

The answer is you can't.

Summary

Let us review:

We reward ignorance equally as we do intelligence

We equate opinion with fact.

We lower the bar of discourse, and then

We put the sociopaths in charge.

As a result, we have a segment of the population that is easily manipulated, quick to war, fickle, with a lowered attention span, short-sighted and highly combustible in their patriotic zeal, passive in their response to over-reaching control and invasion, who will sacrifice true freedom for false security, who are incapable of critical analysis, and who will even take actions that are not in their own self-interest based on the prevailing wind of the moment. These same people, when pushed to defend their beliefs and actions with facts, will invariably default to simply regurgitating the prevailing talking points offered to them by their self-absorbed, sociopathic leaders, or simply resort to.....wait for it...pulling numbers out of their asses...again and again!

20. ❑ "Do you smoke pot?" ❑

[US marijuana use] Daily or almost daily use of marijuana (used on 20 or more days in the past month) increased from 5.1 million persons in 2005 to 2007 to 8.1 million persons in 2013.

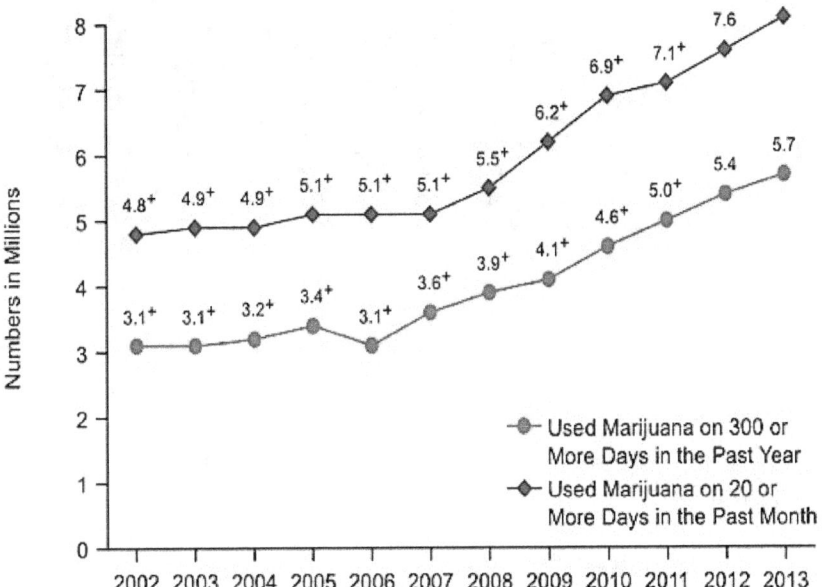

It's safe to say (based on this and other data):
"Marijuana use has increased steadily over the past 5 years."
"Marijuana was the most used illicit drug in 2013."
"64.7% of current illicit drug users used only pot last month."

Source: 2013 National Survey on Drug Use and Health

21. ❑ "SHE is probably a pot head!" ❑

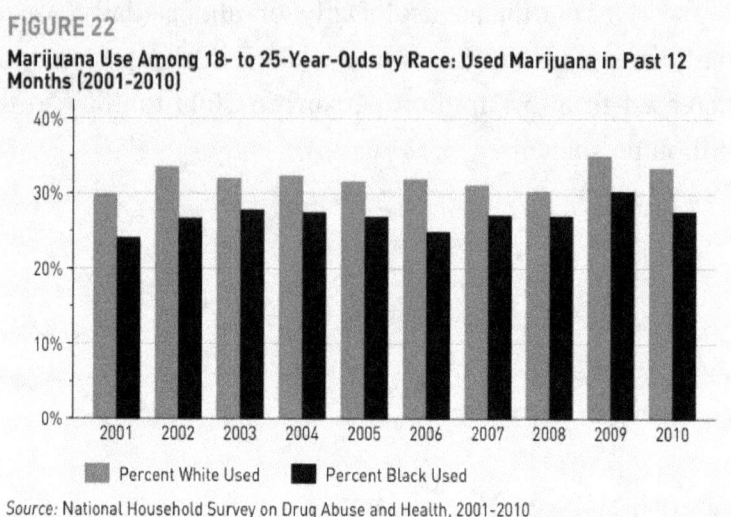

FIGURE 22

Marijuana Use Among 18- to 25-Year-Olds by Race: Used Marijuana in Past 12 Months (2001-2010)

Source: National Household Survey on Drug Abuse and Health, 2001-2010

It's safe to say:

"Between the ages of 18-25, whites used marijuana more than blacks within the past 12 months."

What the numbers don't reveal:

"Even though the rates of use are roughly equivalent between Blacks and Whites, minorities, overwhelmingly, are the ones being arrested: In 2010, the Black arrest rate for marijuana possession was 716 per 100,000, while the white arrest rate was 192 per 100,000. Stated another way, a Black person was 3.73 times more likely to be arrested for marijuana possession than a white person—a disparity that increased 32.7% between 2001 and 2010."

Note: figures will vary based on what age group is polled.

Source: The War on Marijuana in Black & White. The American Civil Liberties Union

22. ☐ "The gays are gettin' married everywhere!" ☐

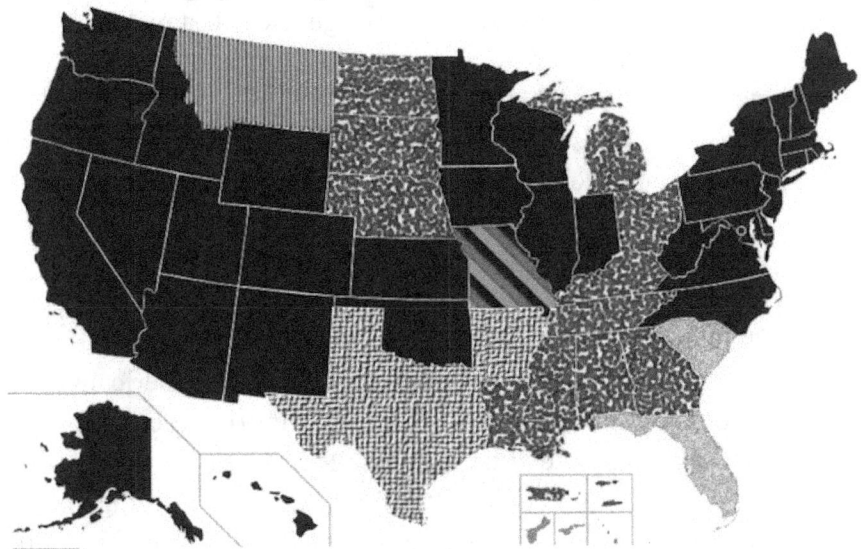

■ Same-sex marriage legal(2)
■ Same-sex marriage performed elsewhere recognized
□ Same-sex marriage legalization pending (3)
□ No prohibition or recognition
▦ Judicial rulings overturning ban stayed pending appeal
▥ Same-sex marriage banned contrary to fed circ precedent
▨ Same-sex marriage banned

LEGAL: In the following 25 states and the District of Columbia: California, Colorado, Connecticut, Delaware, Hawaii, Illinois, Indiana, Iowa, Maine, Maryland, Massachusetts, Minnesota, New Hampshire, New Jersey, New Mexico, New York, Oklahoma, Oregon, Pennsylvania, Rhode Island, Utah, Vermont, Virginia, Washington and Wisconsin.

BANNED: In the following states: Alabama, Alaska, Arizona, Georgia, Kansas, Mississippi, Missouri, Montana, Nebraska, North Carolina, North Dakota, Ohio, South Carolina, South Dakota, Tennessee, West Virginia and Wyoming.

UNDER REVIEW: Courts in these states have declared same-sex marriage bans unconstitutional, but the rulings have been stayed): Arkansas, Florida, Idaho, Kentucky, Louisiana, Michigan, Nevada and Texas.

Source: Wikipedia. Graphic: Lokal_Profil

23. ❑ "Some of my best friends are gay!" ❑

[Random same sex marriage, LGBT statistics]

44% -- Percentage of the U.S. population living in a state that allows same-sex marriage.

2004 -- The year that same-sex marriage became legal in Massachusetts, the first U.S. state to do so.

27% -- Americans who thought same-sex marriage should be legal in 1996, according to a Gallup Poll.

55% -- Americans who think it should be legal in 2014, according to the same poll.

3.5% -- Approximate percentage of Americans who identify as lesbian, gay or bisexual, in 2011 research by the Williams Institute at UCLA, and 2012 Gallup Poll.

10% -- People identifying as LGBT living in the District of Columbia, according to a 2012 Gallup Poll. This is the highest percentage in the country.

1.7% -- People identifying as LGBT living in N Dakota, Gallup (2012); lowest percentage in US.

646,464 -- Same-sex-couple households in the United States in 2010, according to the Census Bureau.

25.3% -- Percentage of same-sex couple households in the United States in 2012 with children living with them, according to the Census Bureau.

"Gay or lesbian adults should have the right to adopt children."			
	Strongly Agree	**Agree**	**Disagree**	**Strongly Disagree**
Female	23.1%	42.3%	20.1%	11.9%
Male	12.9%	41.8%	24.8%	18.1%

Sources: Census Bureau; CDC National Survey of Family Growth

24. ❑ "Mass shootings happen all the time!" ❑

[Mass murder] The FBI's definition of mass murder or mass killing is the slaying of four or more people. Shootings related to drug or gang violence often get less media coverage than those by a crazed gunman.

Mass killings occurred across the U.S. at a rate of about one every two weeks since 2006. Mass *killings* include all methods (gun shootings, stabbings, blunt force and smoke inhalation) and types (family killings, public killing, robbery/burglary and other). Mass *shootings* (a subset) include only public killings by gun.

Year	Mass Killings	Number dead	Mass shooting	Number dead
2006	39	184	4	22
2007	26	148	3	45
2008	36	166	5	26
2009	34	182	4	38
2010	26	121	2	12
2011	29	138	4	23
2012	22	132	6	63
2013	30	137	4	27
2014	17	77	2	10
TOTAL	259	1285	34	266

Related: mental health, gun control, and prescription drugs

CRS Report: Public Mass Shootings in the United States: Selected Implications for Federal Public Health & Safety Policy Mother Jones; Full data
Source: USA TODAY reporting and analysis by Paul Overberg, Meghan Hoyer, Mark Hannan, Jodi Upton, Barbie Hansen and Erin Durkin

25. ❑ "It was a killing spree!" ❑

[Mass shootings of 12 or more] While there's no discernible trend in overall mass killings and shootings, Rachel Maddow presented an analysis (credited to professor Charles Catania at the University of Maryland) that showed that the gun "killing sprees" in which 12 or more people have been killed have, in fact, been on the rise in recent years. Of the 12 killing sprees that occurred from 1949 to 2013, it took 50 years from 1949 to 1999 to reach the halfway point, and only 6 years from 2007 to 2013 to reach the other half.

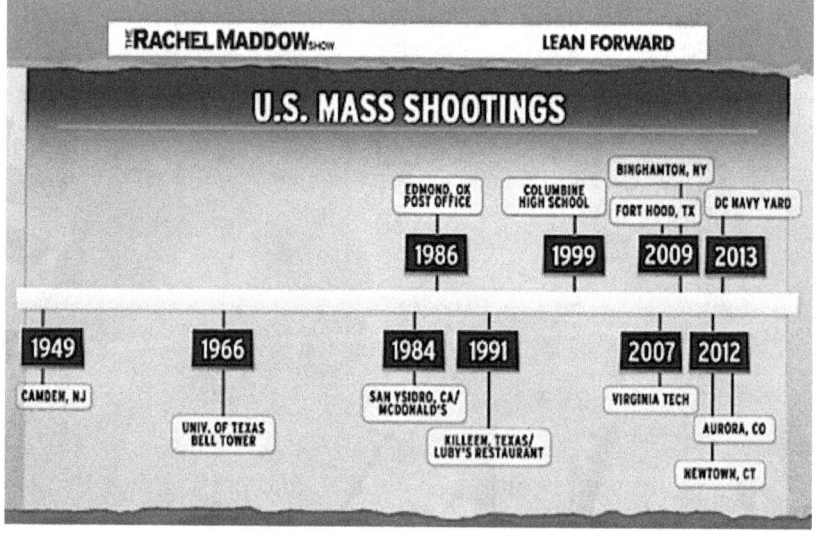

Source: Rachel Maddow

A thought:
Truth is a liberal idea

Truth is a liberal idea.

Of course, truth should *not* be only a liberal idea. Truth should be universal. Neither should science be a liberal idea. Same for the concept of equality. All of these are not and should not be exclusively liberal ideas.

However, when you are a political party in America, and your platform includes (1) rolling back civil rights and (2) denying voting rights, and (3) denying reproductive freedom of choice to women, and (4) opposing gay equality, and (5) closing the borders, and (6) keeping the minimum wage low; then you've positioned yourself in the "against" column for every issue in which the prevailing public trend is "for."

Furthermore, when your platform includes (1) favoring more guns, (2) more religion in schools (3) more jobs sent overseas, then you've positioned yourself in the "for" column for every issue in which the prevailing public wish is "against."

Facts are not liberal. But when your party's primary stances includes (1) denial of climate change, and (2) denial of science in general, then you've positioned yourself counter to the majority of the population.

However, since your platform's agenda is the rollback of freedoms and rights—concepts which any thinking individual wishes to maintain and advance, not relinquish; and if you identify yourself and your platform as "conservative," then those concepts which stand in opposition your party's agenda and championed by the opposition—freedom, choice, science, fact and the will of the majority—become the purview of the "liberals." If you wish to garner support for ideas that run counter to basic freedoms and provable facts, then the only way to accomplish this is to lie to your constituents. There's just no way around it. You can't control a free individual with truth. The only way to control someone is to lie to him. Your party, by default, must then embrace lies as a means of control. In other words, lying (pulling numbers out of your ass) is central to the execution of the conservative agenda, and *truth, by default, becomes a "liberal" idea.*

Yes, to conservatives, this book will appear to be nothing more than a project advancing a liberal agenda. That is true, but not because I am a liberal, nor because the ideas of fact, freedom, proof or science are inherently liberal ideas, but because their opposites have been embraced by conservatives as central to their agenda.

The fact that I say global warming is proved by science does not make me a liberal any more than saying God exists makes me a conservative. It is only in our society's conflation of *science* with *liberalism* and *religion* with *conservatism* that we have assigned these ideological labels to what are really universal concepts.

US
Politics

"[T]he success of democracy depends, in the end, on the reliability of the judgments we citizens make, and hence upon our capacity and determination to weigh arguments and evidence rationally." — **Irving M. Copi**

Legality is not a defense. The term "legal" only has as much meaning as the society allows it to have. It was "legal" at one time to own other human beings. It was "illegal" at one time to marry someone of another race. It was "legal" and even an accepted form of family entertainment to lynch other humans. Legality is an idea, a construct of the people in power. Saying something is wrong or right simply because someone decided it was "legal" or "illegal" is a recipe for enslavement. Right-thinking people— people with a correctly functioning moral and ethical compass—should not be hindered by such constructs. It is necessary to think critically and come to decisions based on other determinants than mere "legality." (from the beyonddebate.org website)

26. ☐ "President Obama is a dictator!" ☐

[Executive Orders] Much has been made of President Obama's issuing of executive orders. The fact of the matter is that of the last 13 presidents, he has signed the third least number of executive orders.

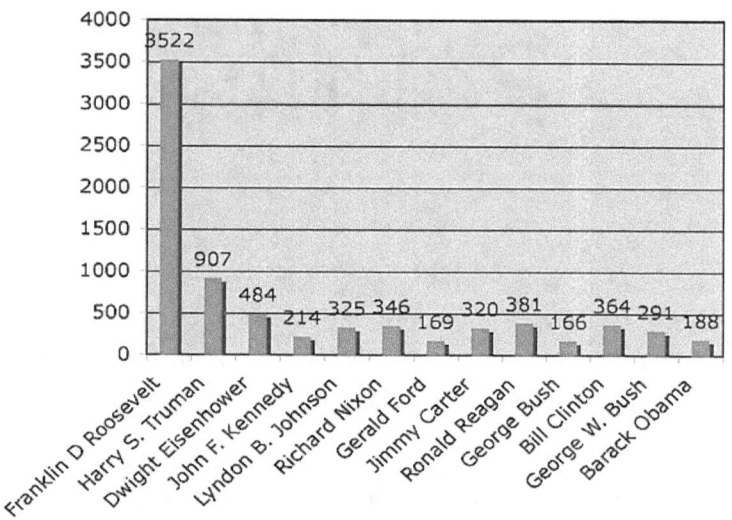

Furthermore, if we compare how many he has signed *per year,* he has actually signed the least:

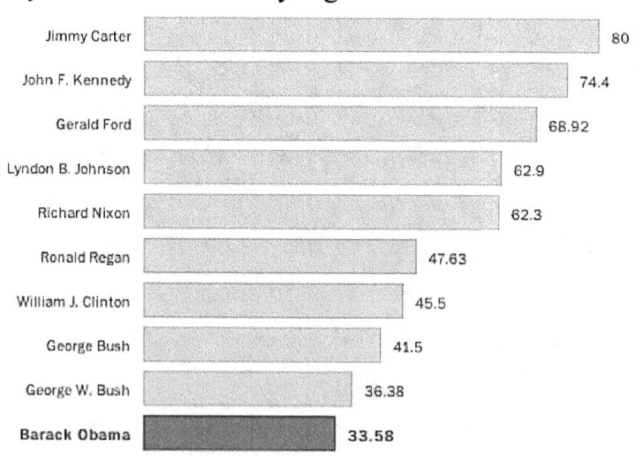

Source: The American Presidency Project

27. ☐ "The 'do nothing' Congress?" ☐

[Congressional bills] In 1948, president Harry Truman scolded then members of the 80th Congress and called them the "do nothing" Congress. That session of Congress' record was 395 "public bills enacted into law" in its first session, and 511 in its second. This current 113th Congress (as of Aug 31, 2014) has achieved 73 and 91. A recent CNN poll revealed 83% of Americans don't approve of the way the current Congress is working, and 65% believe it to be the worst Congress of their lifetime.

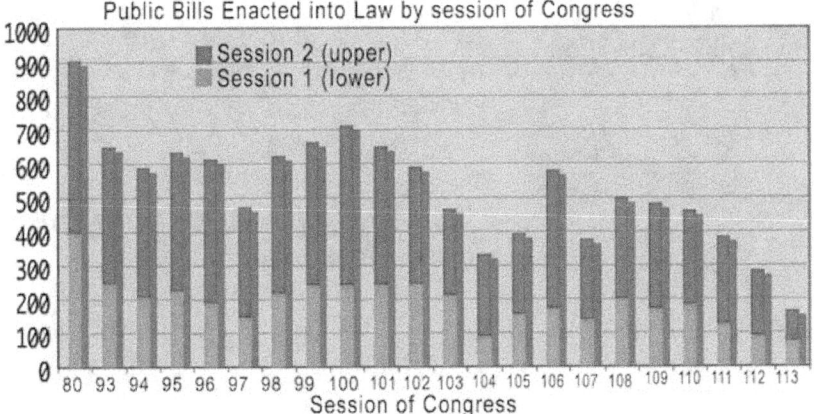

Public Bills Enacted into Law by session of Congress

Congress	Session 1	Session 2
80 (1947-8)	395	511
93 (1973-4)	245	404
94 (1975-6)	205	383
95 (1977-8)	223	411
96 (1979-80)	187	426
97 (1981-2)	145	328
98 (1983-4)	215	408
99 (1985-6)	240	424
100 (1987-8)	240	473
101 (1989-90)	240	410
102 (1991-2)	243	347
103 (1993-4)	210	255
104 (1995-6)	88	245
105 (1997-8)	153	241
106 (1999-2000)	170	410
107 (2001-2)	136	241
108 (2003-4)	198	300
109 (2005-6)	169	313
110 (2007-8)	180	280
111 (2009-10)	125	258
112 (2011-12)	90	193
113 (2013-14)	73*	91*

thru Aug 31, 2014
Sources: Office of the Clerk US House of Representatives.; CNN

28. ☐ "Did he/she really, actually say that???" ☐

[Real quotes] Yes, the exact words were:

"I'm tired of hearing about the minimum wage."--Gov Chris Christie, 2014

"We had no domestic attacks under Bush – we've had one under Obama." -- Rudy Giuliani, Jan 8, 2010

"I hated the gooks. I will hate them as long as I live." John McCain - During the 2004 presidential election

"As for that VP talk all the time, I'll tell you, I still can't answer that question until somebody answers for me what is it exactly that the VP does every day?"—Sarah Palin

"Bomb, bomb bomb, bomb bomb Iran." –John McCain

"Outside of the killings, DC has one of the lowest crime rates in the country."-- Marion Barry, March 24th, 1989

"It all depends on what the meaning of the word 'is' is." -- Bill Clinton during Grand Jury testimony, August, 1998

"Life is indeed precious, and I believe the death penalty helps affirm this fact." – New York mayor Edward Koch

"I'll be long gone before some smart person ever figures out what happened inside this Oval Office."-- George W. Bush, 2008

"I'm not a witch...I'm you." -- Christine O'Donnell *2010*

"I think that gay marriage should be between a man and a woman."-- California Gov. Arnold Schwarzenegger
Sources: Public record

29. ❑ "Which millionaire should I vote for?" ❑

[Congressional net worth] Here is a list of the top 20 wealthiest members of Congress by net worth as of 2014, based on the financial disclosure statements of all 541 senators, representatives and delegates. Their assets include various combinations of investments, real estate, trusts and bank accounts.

1	Rep. Darrell Issa	Republican	CA	$357.25 million
2	Rep. Michael McCaul	Republican	TX	$117.54 million
3	Rep. John Delaney	Democratic	MD	$111.92 million
4	Sen. Jay Rockefeller	Democratic	WV	$108.05 million
5	Sen. Mark Warner	Democratic	VA	$95.13 million
6	Rep. Jared Polis	Democratic	CO	$73.56 million
7	Sen. Rich.Blumenthal	Democratic	CT	$62.06 million
8	Rep. Scott Peters	Democratic	CA	$45.04 million
9	Sen. Dianne Feinstein	Democratic	CA	$43.72 million
10	Rep. Suzan DelBene	Democratic	WA	$37.89 million
11	Rep. Vern Buchanan	Republican	FL	$37.15 million
12	Rep. Chellie Pingree	Democratic	ME	$34.47 million
13	Rep. Gary Miller	Republican	CA	$32.97 million
14	Rep. Nancy Pelosi	Democratic	CA	$29.01 million
15	Rep. James Renacci	Democratic	OH	$28.08 million
16	Rep. Roger Williams	Republican	TX	$28.01 million
17	Rep. Alan Grayson	Democratic	FL	$26.18 million
18	Rep. Chris Collins	Republican	NY	$22.50 million
19	Rep. Rod Frelinghuysen	Republican	NJ	$22.21 million
20	Rep. Diane Black	Republican	TN	$21.24 million

So, next time you're wondering who to vote for, don't worry, you can just ask the millionaire newscasters, talk show hosts and pundits who cover them.

Source: RollCall.com

30. ❏ "Stop voter fraud!" ❏

[Voter fraud statistics] The entire nation of the United States has 2,068 cases of <u>alleged</u> election fraud since 2000. By category (individual's status), "Unknown" had the highest percentage of accused at 31 percent (645 cases), followed by "Voters" at 31 percent (633 cases). The most prevalent fraud was "Absentee Ballot Fraud" at 24 percent (491 cases). The final status of most cases was "Pleaded" at 27 percent (558 cases). Note:

> 513 have not been charged.
> Of those charged, 23 have been found not guilty.
> Of those charged, 93 have been convicted.
> Of those convicted, 25 have been voters while 45

have been either a Campaign Official or Election Official

Type of Accused:
Voter 31.2%
Unknown 29.8%
Campaign Official 19.9%
Election Official 12.9%
Third Party Organizations 6.2%

TYPE OF ACCUSATION
Absentee Ballot Fraud 24.2%
Unknown   19.0%
Registration Fraud   17.8%
Casting Ineligible Vote   13.0%
Double Voting7.4%
Other 6.3%
Petition Fraud 5.9%
Vote Buying   4.8%
Felon Casting Ineligible Vote 3.7%
Non-Citizen Casting Ineligible Vote 2.8%
Campaign Fraud

Sources: Election Fraud Database Project
  Voter Impersonation: 31 credible cases out of 1 billion ballots

A thought:
Why America deserves a
candidate like Mitt Romney

(Originally published August 2012).

As I watch the unfolding of the 2012 presidential campaign in the United States, one of the first things that is obvious to me is that this election campaign is not about policies. You might think that all these debates about abortion, right to life, tax reform, Medicare, etc., are all policy debates, but support of the Republican party by people other than the framers of the party's policies themselves is not based on the soundness, ethics or ultimate value or benefit of those policies, but something else entirely. For if it were about the policies, it would defy reason and logic that people would support and vote for politicians who advocate such extreme and demonstrably detrimental policies.

If you are a woman, for example, you would have to be insane to vote for a party that deprives you of control of your body and would–if that's not what you desired–force you to bear a child that is the result of rape or incest.

If you are an immigrant (particularly a Spanish-speaking one), you would have to be insane to vote for a party with policies that target you as a problem to be fixed and essentially want you to "self-deport."

If you are black, you would have to be insane to vote for a party whose policies demonize you as the cause of America's economic and moral downfall.

And, in fact, we know, based on recent polling, that support for Mitt Romney, the Republican candidate for president, is down among women, among Latinos (the nation's largest immigrant group), and among blacks.

So, who is supporting the Republicans? Well, it's primarily whites. Not all whites, of course, but whites of a certain era, worldview, mindset and the children they raise.

Now, for the record, when I say "the Republicans," I'm not referring to people within the general public who claim to be Republicans. I'm referring to the party leaders themselves who set and make policy. I make that distinction because there really is no Republican party anymore. There are people (like Todd Akin, Paul Ryan, Bob McDonnell, et.al) with extreme agendas who are simply using the title, identity and ballot space formerly belonging to the Republican Party to advance those agendas. (It's easier to hijack a party in a two-party system, than to create a third party). And then, there are the people who follow them.

But what's equally obvious and beyond debate is that those Republicans don't have their followers' best interests at heart. When the Republicans send jobs overseas, their followers suffer. When the republicans give tax breaks to the wealthy while taxing the poor, it's their followers who suffer. When the Republicans wage war on women, it's their followers who suffer.

How could they be so blind as to not see what's happening? How can they not see how they are being used? Well, they can't see it because, as I said, this campaign is not about issues. It's about being anti-Obama. The Republicans are using their followers' fear and racially steeped hatred to further an agenda that will ultimately benefit the Republicans themselves, but not their followers.

So, as I watch the ardent support and enthusiasm from within the ranks of those followers who will ultimately suffer at the very hands of the policy-makers and policies they endorse and support, I can't help but think: "it would serve them right!"

For those Republicans who have manufacturing jobs, it would serve them right to vote a guy in who will continue in his Bain tradition and send their jobs overseas for his personal benefit. But they can't see that, because their support is not based on his history, track record or policies. It's simply about their fear and hatred of Obama.

For those Republicans who are of retirement age, it would serve them right to have a president who will roll back Medicare. But they can't see that, because their support is not based on his history, track record or policies. It's simply about their fear and hatred of Obama.

For those Republicans who are women, it would serve them right to have a president who will reverse Roe v. Wade, outlaw abortions in cases of rape and incest and force women to have ultrasounds and see the fetus when contemplating abortion. But they can't see that, because their support is not based on his history, track record or policies. It's simply about their fear and hatred of Obama.

If the lies are believed; if the voter suppression tactics work; if the anti-Obama hatred is greater than common sense among those who believe the lies and whose votes are cast, then Mitt Romney will become president of the United States in November 2012. It would serve them right. However, that's not a mature view to hold, for all of us would suffer. (In a future post, I'll tell you why that actually will not happen–why Romney will not be elected–) but for now here's what's beyond debate:

Because the Republican Party no longer exists, you can't have a debate about issues because those who follow the party at this stage are not following the party based on issues, but based on emotion (or naiveté). The media has no choice but to grant both sides legitimacy in their coverage and must pretend as if the electorate's support for the current republican candidate is based on legitimate policy differences. You, however, are not required to. You can see things as they are, and get beyond debate.

Graphic source: Funnyshirts.org

Education

"An education isn't how much you have committed to memory, or even how much you know. It's being able to differentiate between what you know and what you don't"-- Anatole France

It is the mark of an educated mind to be able to entertain a thought without accepting it. "--Aristotle

The goal of education is the advancement of knowledge and the dissemination of truth. "--John F. Kennedy

Don't limit a child to your own learning, for he was born in another time. "--Rabindranath Tagore

Poor people cannot rely on the government to come to help you in times of need. You have to get your education. Then nobody can control your destiny. "--Charles Barkley

Education is a progressive discovery of our own ignorance. "--Will Durant

The paradox of education is precisely this--that as one begins to become conscious, one begins to examine the society in which he is being educated. " ---James A. Baldwin

If the education of our kids comes from radio, television, newspapers--if that's where they get the most of their knowledge, and not from the schools, then the powers that be are definitely in charge because they own all those outlets. "--Maynard James Keenan

31. ❑ "Shouldn't you be in school right now?" ❑

[School attendance] In fall 2014:

49.8 million students will attend public elementary and secondary schools.

1.3 million children will attend public prekindergarten

4.1 million students are expected to enroll in 9th grade

35.1 million will be in prekindergarten through grade 8

14.7 million will be in grades 9 through 12.

5.0 million students are expected to attend private schools

24.8 million will be white (The national percentage of whites is projected to be less than 50 percent in 2014)

7.7 million will be Black students,

12.8 million will be Hispanic students,

2.6 million will be Asian/Pacific Islander students,

0.5 million will be American Indian/Alaska Native

1.4 million will be of two or more races

The public school systems will employ about 3.1 million full-time-equivalent (FTE) teachers in fall 2014, the pupil/teacher ratio—will be 16 to 1.

In 2011–12, there were about 13,600 public school districts (source) with over 98,300 public schools, including about 5,700 charter schools.

Source: National Center for Education Statistics

32. ❏ "How important are my SAT scores?" ❏

[SAT scores] 1,672,395 students from the class of 2014 took the SAT, an increase compared to 1,660,047 students last year.

Nearly half were minority students: 47.5% (793,986 students), an increase from 45.9% in 2013.

The Benchmark score of 1550 is associated with a 65% probability of obtaining a first-year GPA of B- or higher at a four-year college. Only 42.6% met the SAT College and Career Readiness Benchmark;

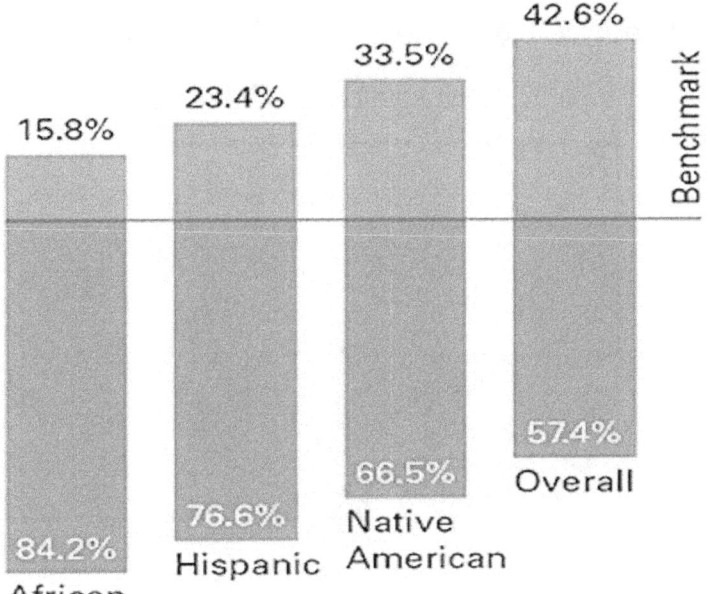

Of students who meet the benchmark: 78% enrolled in a four-year college or university, compared to only 46% of those who did not meet the benchmark.

Of students who meet the benchmark: 54% earned a bachelor's degree within four years, compared to only 27% of those who did not meet the benchmark.

Source: The College Board Performance Statistics

33. ❏ "I owe so much in student loans!" ❏
[Student debt]

1. American borrowers owe $1.2 trillion in federal student debt (source: *Consumer Financial Protection Bureau*)

2. The average undergraduate borrower from the class of 2012 took on between $27,183 and $29,400 in student loan debt, according to the 1,006 schools that submitted data to U.S. News in an annual survey.

3. Only 41 percent of students graduate in four years.

4. The 3-year loan default rate is 15% for recent graduates.

5. Borrowers older than 60 owe $43 billion in loan debt.

Average Debt Over Time[1]

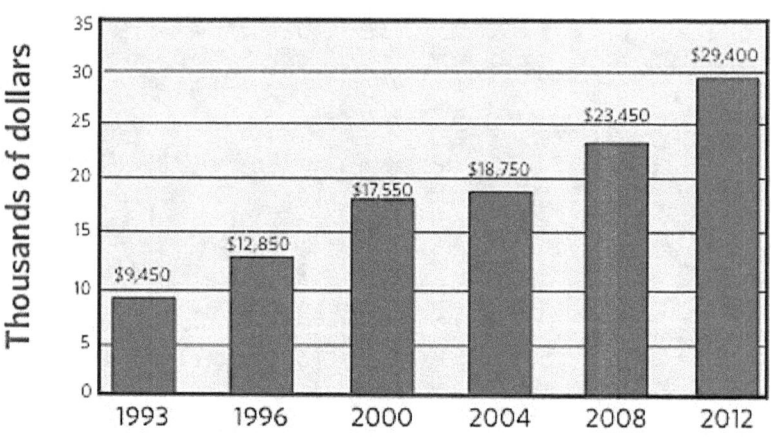

[1]*Figures are for graduating seniors with loans. In 1993, 47% of students graduated with loans; this figure rose to 59% in 1996, 64% in 2000, 65% in 2004, 68% in 2008, and 71% in 2012.*

*Source: US News & World Report
Project on Student Debt*

34. ❑ "Get an education to earn more money." ❑

[Education vs. salary]. Here is a chart showing mean annual earnings as a function of degree earned.

Characteristic	Total persons	Mean earnings by level of highest degree (dollars)						
		Not a high school graduate	High school graduate only	Some college, no degree	Asso- ciate's	Bach- elor's	Master's	Profes- sional	Doctorate
All persons [1]........	**42,469**	**20,241**	**30,627**	**32,295**	**39,771**	**56,665**	**73,738**	**127,803**	**103,054**
Age:									
25 to 34 years old	36,595	19,415	27,511	31,392	35,544	45,692	58,997	86,440	74,626
35 to 44 years old	49,356	24,728	33,614	39,806	42,353	65,346	80,593	136,366	108,147
45 to 54 years old	51,956	23,725	36,090	44,135	46,413	69,548	86,532	148,805	112,134
55 to 64 years old	50,372	24,537	34,583	42,547	42,192	59,670	76,372	149,184	110,895
65 years old and over ...	37,544	19,395	28,469	29,602	33,541	44,147	45,138	95,440	95,585
Sex:									
Male...............	50,186	23,036	35,468	39,204	47,572	69,479	90,964	150,310	114,347
Female..............	33,797	15,514	24,304	25,340	33,432	43,589	58,534	89,897	83,708
White [2]..............	43,337	20,457	31,429	33,119	40,632	57,762	73,771	127,942	104,533
Male...............	51,287	23,353	36,418	40,352	48,521	71,286	91,776	149,149	115,497
Female..............	34,040	15,187	24,615	25,537	33,996	43,309	58,036	89,526	85,682
Black [2]..............	33,362	18,936	26,970	29,129	33,734	47,799	60,067	102,328	82,510
Male...............	37,553	21,828	30,723	33,969	41,142	55,655	68,890	(B)	(B)
Female..............	29,831	15,644	22,964	25,433	29,464	42,587	54,523	(B)	(B)
Hispanic [3]..............	29,565	19,816	25,998	29,836	33,783	49,017	71,322	79,228	88,435
Male...............	32,279	21,588	28,908	35,089	38,768	58,570	80,737	(B)	89,956
Female..............	25,713	16,170	21,473	24,281	29,785	39,566	61,843	(B)	(B)

Summary of Average:
No high school diploma: $20,241
High school graduate only: $30,627
Some college: $32,294
Associate's Degree: $39,771
Bachelor's Degree: $56,665
Master's: $73,738
Professional: $127,803
Doctorate: $103,054

Source:
US Census Educational Attainment by Selected Characteristics (2010)

35. ❑ "Why is an education so expensive???" ❑

[Countries with free education] Not all countries charge exorbitantly for education. Here are seven countries that will provide a good education for free or almost free:

1. *Brazil*: Brazil's universities charge registration fees, notes, but they do not require regular tuition. Many of them also offer courses in English.

2. *Germany*: Germany has 900 programs in English, and is eager to attract foreign students to tuition-free universities due to the country's shortage of skilled workers.

3. *Finland*: Finland doesn't have tuition fees, but the government does warn foreigners that they have to cover living expenses.

4. *France*: France does charge tuition – but normally around 200 dollars at public universities.

5. *Norway*: Norwegian students, including foreigners studying in the country, do not have to pay any college tuition. Be forewarned, however, of the harsh winters and high cost of living.

6. *Slovenia*: Slovenia has 150 English-language programs, and only charges a registration fee – no tuition.

7. *Sweden*: Sweden has over 300 English-language programs. Although college there is free, cost of living may be pricey for foreigners.

Source: Washington Post

And while we're on the topic of life in the wider world…

The
World

"Statistically speaking, in China, even if you are a one in a million kind of guy, there are a thousand more just like you."

"That's why I felt so at home when I went to Africa. It didn't matter that I was halfway around the world in a foreign country, because all those elements are universal. And I think that's one thing about my work: it's universal."
—Herb Ritts, photographer

"When you travel, remember that a foreign country is not designed to make you comfortable. It is designed to make its own people comfortable."—Clifton Fadiman

"I don't see myself moving back. It's not that I hate the United States. I just always thought it would be a shame not to live in a foreign country."--David Sedaris

36. ❑ "It's a big world out there!" ❑

[World statistics] The world's total population today is already in excess of 7.2 billion, and growing at a faster rate than previously estimated. Revised estimates suggest that world population is likely to reach 9.6 billion by 2050 – 0.3 billion larger than under earlier UN projections.

Asia is the most populous continent, with 4.3 billion or 60% of the world population. The two most populated countries, China and India, hold 37% of the world population. Africa is the second most populated continent, with approx 1 billion (15% of world's population).

25 per cent of the world's 233 countries hold 90 per cent of the population (UNDESA, 2013). Half of all future population growth is expected to occur in just eight countries: Nigeria, India, Tanzania, the Democratic Republic of Congo (DRC), Niger, Uganda, Ethiopia and the USA (UNDESA, 2013b). Of these countries, Nigeria will experience the most growth, and is expected to become the third most populous country in the world by 2050 (behind China and India).

The median age of the world's population was estimated to be 29.7 years in 2014.

Total annual births were highest in the late 1980s at about 138 million/year and are expected to remain constant at their 2011 level of 134 million/YWe, while deaths number 56 million per year, and are expected to increase to 80 million per year by 2040.

Source: United Nations

37. ❑ "My country is bigger than yours!" ❑

[Country size vs. Africa] This clever map by Kai Krause was
created to make a simple point: "Africa is so mind-numbingly

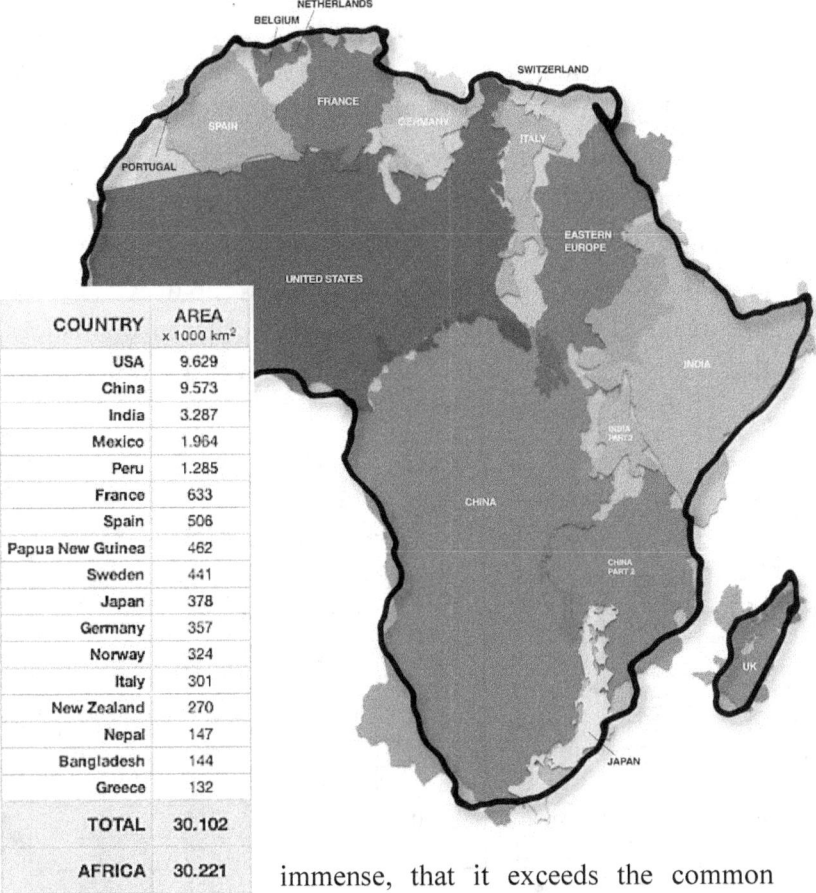

COUNTRY	AREA x 1000 km²
USA	9.629
China	9.573
India	3.287
Mexico	1.964
Peru	1.285
France	633
Spain	506
Papua New Guinea	462
Sweden	441
Japan	378
Germany	357
Norway	324
Italy	301
New Zealand	270
Nepal	147
Bangladesh	144
Greece	132
TOTAL	**30.102**
AFRICA	**30.221**
Just for reference: Surface of the Moon	37.930

immense, that it exceeds the common
assumptions by just about anyone I ever
met: it contains the *entirety of the USA,
all of China, India,* as well as *Japan* and pretty much *all of
Europe* as well - *all combined!"* Because of the distortions in
actual size that result from the standard Mercator projection map
that was used to teach most of us basic geography, Africa is just
about always hugely underestimated - even by college grads, by
a factor of 2 or 3. Read the fascinating story of how Kai's map
went viral at http://kai.subblue.com/en/africa.html

38. ❑ "What's the best country to live?" ❑

[The Social Progress Index] ranks 132 countries not on GDP (Gross Domestic Product; i.e. economy), but on how well each provides (a) Basic Human Needs (Nutrition & basic medical care, water & sanitation, shelter & personal safety), (b) Foundations of Wellbeing (access to basic knowledge, access to information and communication, health & wellness, and ecosystem sustainability), and (c) Opportunity (Personal rights, personal freedom & choice, tolerance & inclusion, access to advanced education); in other words, based on factors that really matter to people. The Top 20 for each criteria are:

	Basi Need		Well being		Oppor tunity		SP Index
Denmark	95.73	Switzerl	89.78	NZeal	88.01	N Zeal	88.24
Switzerla	94.87	Iceland	88.19	Canada	87.02	Switzerl	88.19
Japan	94.72	Netherla	87.56	Australia	85.54	Iceland	88.07
Finland	94.63	Norway	86.94	Ireland	82.63	Netherl	87.37
Sweden	94.59	Austria	86.35	US	82.54	Norway	87.12
Austria	94.57	NZeala	84.97	UK	82.29	Sweden	87.08
Iceland	94.32	German	84.96	Sweden	81.95	Canada	86.95
Netherlan	93.91	Denmark	84.82	Finland	81.92	Finland	86.91
Ireland	93.63	Sweden	84.71	Iceland	81.71	Denmar	86.55
Norway	93.59	Estonia	84.39	Norway	80.82	Australi	86.10
Canada	93.52	Finland	84.17	Netherl	80.63	Austria	85.11
Germany	93.08	Slovenia	83.60	Switzerla	79.92	German	84.61
Belgium	92.74	Czech R	83.26	Denmark	79.10	UK	84.56
Australia	92.47	Slovakia	83.25	Japan	78.67	Japan	84.21
Slovenia	92.05	Poland	81.10	Belgium	76.34	Ireland	84.05
UK	91.90	osta Rica	80.53	German	75.81	US	82.77
Czech Re	91.77	Canada	80.31	Spain	75.19	Belgium	82.63
NZealand	91.74	Australia	80.27	Uruguay	74.56	Slovenia	81.65
France	91.23	UK	79.47	Portugal	74.43	Estonia	81.28
Portugal	90.93	France	79.37	Austria	74.42	France	81.11

Keep in mind that these indices may not apply to immigrants and foreigners living in these countries.

Source: The Social Progress Index

39. ❑ "Who's got the highest immigration?" ❑

[Net immigration] is the number of new immigrants per 1,000 people. A positive number means more people are coming in than leaving. A negative number means more people are leaving than entering. Here are the top 40 (2012) Here are the bottom 20:

1	Lebanon	83.82	21	St Maarten	6.63
2	Qatar	27.35	22	Djibouti	6.06
3	Zimbabwe	21.78	23	Australia	5.74
4	Brit Virg Isl	17.69	24	Canada	5.66
5	Jordan	17.22	25	Sweden	5.46
6	Libya	16.01	26	Switzerland	5.43
7	Cayman Isl	14.71	27	Liechtenstein	4.72
8	Singapore	14.55	28	Botswana	4.62
9	Bahrain	13.6	29	Italy	4.29
10	UAE	13.58	30	Jersey	4.08
11	Anguilla	12.43	31	N Caledonia	4.06
12	Turks & Carac	12.23	32	Nepal	3.71
13	South Sudan	11.94	33	Macau	3.4
14	Cyprus	9.89	34	Ireland	3.31
15	Aruba	9.04	35	Monaco	2.85
16	San Marino	8.31	36	Portugal	2.74
17	Luxembourg	7.97	37	Yemen	2.61
18	Norway	7.96	38	UK	2.56
19	Spain	7.24	39	Brunei	2.47
20	Isle of Man	6.84	40	USA	2.45

Source: CIA World Factbook

203	Fiji	-6.86	213	St Vincent	-9.60
204	Congo	-7.02	214	Guyana	-9.67
205	Guam	-7.61	215	Moldova	-9.80
206	Lesotho	-7.62	216	Samoa	-10.12
207	US Virgin Isl	-7.84	217	Maldives	-12.67
208	El Salvador	-8.44	218	Nauru	-14.12
209	St Pierre/Miquelon	-8.57	219	Tonga	-17.85
210	Sao Tome/Princip	-8.79	220	Micronesia FSM	-20.93
211	Puerto Rico	-8.93	221	Am Samoa	-21.64
212	Somalia	-9.51	222	Syria	-113.51

40. ❑ "Who's killing its citizens?" ❑

[State sponsored executions] Countries and the number of their citizens executed in 2012 as determined by Amnesty International.

Country	Executions
China	2000+
Iran	314+
Iraq	129+
Saudi Arabia	79+
USA	43
Yemen	28+
Sudan	19+
Afghanistan	14
Gambia	9
Japan	7
North Korea	6+
Palestine	6
Somalia	6+
South Sudan	5+
Belarus	3+
Pakistan	1
UAE	1+
Bangladesh	1
India	1

Source: "Death Sentences & Executions 2012." Amnesty International.

41. ❏ "YOU people are so articulate!" ❏

[Most educated countries] The Organization for Economic Cooperation and Development's (OECD) *Education at a Glance 2012* report calculated the proportion of residents with a college or college equivalent degree in the group's 34 member nations and other major economies. Based on the report, 24/7 Wall St. identified the 10 countries with the highest proportion of adults with a college degree.

Country	% pop	Avg growth	GDP per cap
Canada	51%	2.4%	$39,050
Israel	46%	n/a	$26,531
Japan	45%	2.9%	$33,785
US	42%	1.3%	$46,548
N Zealand	41%	3.5%	$29,711
S Korea	40%	5.2%	$28,797
UK	38%	4.0%	$35,756
Finland	38%	1.4%	$36,307
Australia	38%	3.2%	$40,790
Ireland	37%	7.3%	$40,478

Canada is the only nation where more than half of all adults had a tertiary education in 2010. This was up from 40% of the adult population in 2000, when the country also ranked as the world's most educated. Canada has managed to become a world leader in education without being a leader in education spending, which totaled just 6.1% of GDP in 2009, or less than the 6.3% average for the OECD.

Sources: *OECD Statistics* (GDP, unemployment, income, population, labour, education, trade, finance, prices..) 247WallSt

42. ❑ "Is it easy to get a job there?"❑

[Global Unemployment] Total unemployment rate

1	Cambodia	0.0		41	St Kitts N	4.5		81	Philippine	7.4
2	Qatar	0.3		42	Iceland	4.5		82	Argentina	7.5
3	Thailand	0.7		43	Honduras	4.5		83	Fiji	7.6
4	Guernsey	0.9		44	Luxmbrg	4.9		84	Venzuela	7.9
5	Belarus	1.0		45	Mexico	4.9		85	Cos Rica	7.9
6	Vietnam	1.3		46	Austria	4.9		86	Cen Afr	8.0
7	Vanuatu	1.7		47	Uzbkstan	4.9		87	Bermuda	8.0
8	Jersey	1.7		48	Bngldesh	5.0		88	Ukraine	8.0
9	Macau	1.8		49	Sri Lanka	5.1		89	Anguilla	8.0
10	PapuaN	1.9		50	Burma	5.2		90	Sweden	8.1
11	Laos	1.9		51	Kzkhstan	5.3		91	Finland	8.1
12	Singapor	1.9		52	Germany	5.3		92	Guam	8.2
13	Kiribati	2.0		53	Australia	5.7		93	Mauritius	8.3
14	Seychell	2.0		54	Brazil	5.7		94	Nethrlnds	8.3
15	Monaco	2.0		55	Russia	5.8		95	Kyrgzstn	8.6
16	Isle Man	2.0		56	Israel	5.8		96	BrVirgin	8.7
17	Bhutan	2.1		57	Moldova	5.8		97	Belgium	8.8
18	Lchtnstn	2.3		58	Trinidad	5.9		98	India	8.8
19	Emirates	2.4		59	Denmark	6.0		99	Mongolia	9.0
20	Tajikistan	2.5		60	Azrbaijan	6.0		100	Surinam	9.0
21	Brunei	2.6		61	Montsrrat	6.0		101	Turkey	9.3
22	Gibraltar	3.0		62	Chile	6.0		102	Gmland	9.4
23	Malaysia	3.1		63	USVirg Is	6.2		103	Morcco	9.5
24	HKong	3.1		64	I Salvdr	6.3		104	Colmbia	9.7
25	Switzerl	3.2		65	Malta	6.4		105	Latvia	9.8
26	KoreaS	3.2		66	N Zealnd	6.4		106	S Mquln	9.9
27	Kuwait	3.4		67	Uruguay	6.5		107	Turk C	10.0
28	Norway	3.6		68	Pakistan	6.6		108	France	10.2
29	Peru	3.6		69	Paraguay	6.6		109	Poland	10.3
30	Andorra	4.0		70	Indonesia	6.6		110	Algeria	10.3
31	Caymans	4.0		71	Faroe Is	6.8		111	EU	10.5
32	China	4.1		72	Aruba	6.9		112	Arabia	10.5
33	Taiwan	4.1		73	S Marino	7.0		113	Hngary	10.5
34	Japan	4.1		74	Czech R	7.1		114	Estnia	10.9
35	Guatema	4.1		75	Canada	7.1		115	Antigu	11.0
36	Falkland	4.1		76	UK	7.2		116	Ghana	11.0
37	Palau	4.2		77	Nicargua	7.2		117	Guyna	11.0
38	Ecuador	4.2		78	Romania	7.3		118	CNMI	11.2
39	Cuba	4.3		79	US	7.3		119	Brbdos	11.4
40	Panama	4.5		80	Bolivia	7.4		120	Blgaria	11.6

121	Fr Poly	11.7	151	Tunisia	17.2	181	Camroon	30.0
122	Niue	12.0	152	Armnia	17.3	182	Libya	30.0
123	St Mrtn	12.0	153	Cyprus	17.4	183	Mali	30.0
124	W Ftna	12.2	154	Ethpia	17.5	184	Maurtn	30.0
125	Italy	12.4	155	Syria	17.8	185	Kosov	30.9
126	Lithun	12.4	156	Btswn	17.8	186	Grnda	33.5
127	Curcao	13.0	157	Timor	18.4	187	Afgnst	35.0
128	Tonga	13.0	158	St Vnc	18.8	188	Yemen	35.0
129	Cook Isl	13.1	159	Mntngr	19.1	189	Marshal	36.0
130	Slvnia	13.1	160	Cmros	20.0	190	Kenya	40.0
131	Egypt	13.4	161	Lucia	20.0	191	Swaz	40.0
132	Ireland	13.5	162	Sudan	20.0	192	Haiti	40.6
133	Jordan	14.0	163	Serbia	20.1	193	os Hz	44.3
134	St Hel	14.0	164	Ca Vrd	21.0	194	Nepal	46.0
135	Slvakia	14.4	165	Gabon	21.0	195	Snegal	48.0
136	Bhrain	15.0	166	Croatia	21.6	196	Congo	53.0
137	D Rep	15.0	167	Micro	22.0	197	Djibuti	59.0
138	Georgia	15.0	168	Guinea	22.3	198	Cocos	60.0
139	Oman	15.0	169	W Bnk	22.5	199	Turkn	60.0
140	Zambia	15.0	170	Gaza	22.5	200	Burk Fas	77.0
141	Belize	15.5	171	Dmnca	23.0	201	Liberia	85.0
142	Iran	16.0	172	Nigeria	23.9	202	Nauru	90.0
143	Iraq	16.0	173	S Afric	24.9	203	Zmbab	95.0
144	Pr Rico	16.0	174	Lestho	25.0			
145	Bahamas	16.2	175	Spain	26.3			
146	Jamaica	16.3	176	Namba	27.4			
147	Portgal	16.8	177	Greec	27.9			
148	Albnia	16.9	178	Maldvs	28.0			
149	Mzmb	17.0	179	Mcdna	28.6			
150	Caldna	17.1	180	Samoa	29.8			

Source: <u>*CIA.gov*</u>

43. ❏ "Do they smoke pot there?" ❏

[Marijuana use] Here is a random sampling of countries with some of the highest and lowest lifetime use of marijuana. The figures display what percentage of the population from roughly the ages of 15-64 have used marijuana at some point in their lives.

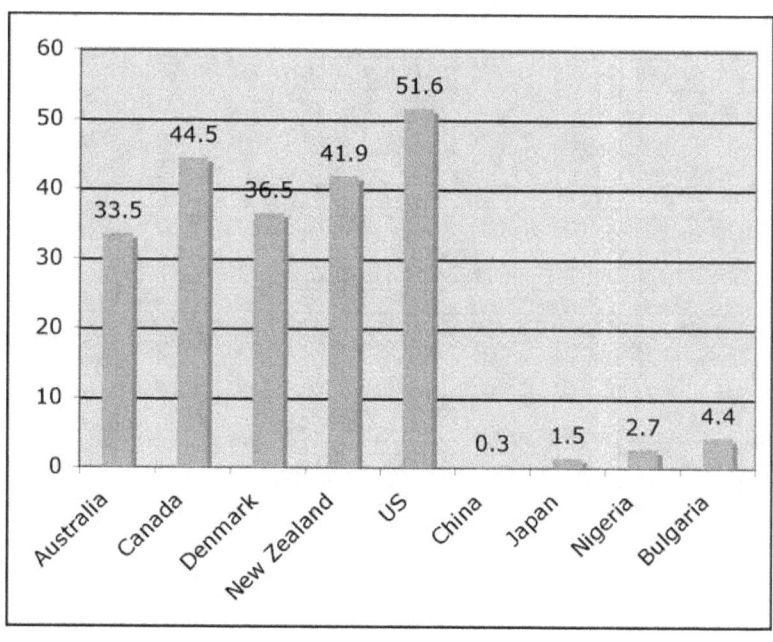

Source: European Monitoring Centre for Drugs & Drug Addiction

44. ❏ "Yeah, but can you buy pot legally there?" ❏

[Legal pot use by country] Two countries where the possession, sale, transport and cultivation of marijuana are completely legal are: North Korea and Uruguay. Marijuana possession is technically illegal, but the possession, sale transport and cultivation have been decriminalized and thus tolerated to varying degrees in the following countries:

Country	Possession	Sale	Transport	Cultivation
Netherland	decriminalized for personal use Legal in smoking areas	Illegal (Legal for coffeeshops)	Illegal (but for coffee shops not enforced)	Illegal (exceptions for personal use)
Portugal	Illegal (decriminalized)	Illegal	Illegal (decriminalized)	Illegal (decriminalized)
Czech Republic	Illegal (decriminalized)	Illegal (purchase legal;	Illegal (decriminalized)	Illegal (decriminalized)
Spain	Illegal (decriminalized)	Illegal	Illegal	Illegal
Peru	Illegal (decriminalized)	Illegal	Illegal decriminalized	Illegal (decriminalized)
Ecuador	Illegal (decriminalized)	Illegal	Illegal	Illegal
Jamaica	Illegal (tentatively decriminalized)	Illegal tentatively decriminalized	Illegal	Illegal (tentatively decriminalized)
Cambodia	Illegal (decriminalized)	Illegal decriminalized	Illegal (decriminal	Illegal (decriminalized)

Source: Wikipedia

45. ❑ "Do they perform same sex marriages?" ❑

[Same sex marriage globally] 17 countries currently recognize same sex marriages. The Netherlands was the first to legalize same-sex marriages, (performed on 1 April 2001). Since then, same-sex marriages have been performed legally by Belgium (2003), Spain (2005), Canada (2003 - in some provinces; 2005 - nationally), South Africa (2006), Norway (2009), Sweden (2009), Portugal (2010), Iceland (2010), Argentina (2010), Denmark (2012), Brazil (2013), France (2013), Uruguay (2013), New Zealand (2013), and the UK (2014, excluding Northern Ireland), and Luxembourg (as of 1 Jan 2015).

Countries where same sex marriage is illegal in some areas and not in others: Mexico, United States.
Countries that offer many rights to same-sex couples but stop short of marriage include Ecuador, Finland, Germany, Greenland, Hungary, Ireland, and Scotland.

Countries that offer some spousal rights to same-sex couples include: Andorra, Austria, Colombia, Croatia, Czech Republic, Liechtenstein, Slovenia, and Switzerland.

Countries that recognize marriages between same-sex couples performed in other countries: Israel and Mexico.

Several Australian states have created lesser mechanisms of status, called "relationship register" or "civil partnership."

In Colombia, same-sex couples in the state will soon be able to register their unions in court.

Source: Freedom to Marry

46. ❑ "Do they have freedom of speech there?" ❑

[Freedom of speech] is the concept of the inherent human right to voice one's opinion publicly without fear of censorship or punishment. "Speech" is not limited to public speaking and is generally taken to include other forms of expression. The right is preserved in the United Nations Universal Declaration of Human Rights and is granted formal recognition by the laws of most nations. Nonetheless the degree to which the right is upheld in practice varies greatly from one nation to another.[Wiki]

The following countries were ranked by TheRichest.com as having the greatest degree of freedom of speech:

10. *Jamaica:* At number ten as of 2014 is Jamaica, which has undergone something of a revelation in terms of the popularization of freedom of speech in the last four years. In late 2010 Miss Jamaica World 2010 and Harvard Law School graduate Chantal Raymond established a blog, freespeechjamaica.com, which aimed to create awareness/public forum for the issue.

9. *Chile*, 8. *Uruguay*, 7. *Portugal*, 6. *Estonia*, 5. *USA*, 4. *Japan*, 3. *United Kingdom*, 2. *Australia*, and....

1. *New Zealand*! The number one country for freedom of speech is New Zealand. The 1990 Bill of Rights act states *"everyone has the right to freedom of expression, including the freedom to seek, receive, and impart information and opinions of any kind in any form."* The country ranks 8th in the Press Freedom Index.

Source: TheRichest.com

A thought:
Freedom of speech does not exist!

In my opinion, people have misinterpreted the concept of free speech.

1. First of all, just because speech is "free," doesn't mean anyone is interested in what you have to say.

2. Secondly, just because speech is "free," doesn't mean your opinions are worth debating. The trouble with our "free" society is this insane yet pervasive and persistent idea that all opinions are equal. Opinions may be equal quantitatively, as in, you have one opinion, and I have another, and therefore $1 = 1$, but *qualitatively*, your idea may be horse puckie!

3. Thirdly, the concept of "free speech" simply means there are no laws on the books that will be used to punish you; and for a country ostensibly governed by the "rule of law" that's a good thing. However, freedom of speech does *not* mean you have freedom from *consequences*. The universe is governed by the law of cause and effect. Just because you are *legally* protected, doesn't mean there are no consequences to your speech.

People will react and respond to the things you say. For instance, upon discovering the truth behind the conditions of meat industry, Oprah had the freedom to say on her show *"It has just stopped me cold from eating another burger!"* There were consequences. She was sued by a lobby of Texas cattle ranchers!

Talk show host, Rush Limbaugh, had the freedom to say on his show what he did about Sandra Fluke. He experienced the public backlash. House Representative Todd Akin had the freedom to opine on the logistics of "legitimate rape." His freely spoken opinion was acted upon by the voting public. The NRA's Wayne LaPierre has the freedom to advocate for more guns in society. However, his position is marginalizing him in the public dialogue. History is replete with examples of people who paid a price for speaking freely: Martin Luther King, Jr., Malcolm X, John Kennedy, et.al.

Those last few examples should not be interpreted in any way as intended to discourage you from speaking freely for what you believe in. My point is simply this: There is nowhere on the planet or in this universe where speech is really free. Your words, whether positive or negative, good or evil—and whether you pull them out of your ass or from somewhere else—always have creative power as well as consequences. Use them wisely!

Sources: PBS Transcript of Oprah episode

47. ❑ "Who's got the most guns?"❑

[Gun ownership per 100 people.]

Country	Guns per 100	Rank
United States	90.0	1
Serbia	58.2	2
Yemen	54.8	3
Switzerland	45.7	4
Finland	45.3	5
Cyprus	36.1	6
Saudi Arabia	35	7
Iraq	34.2	8
Uruguay	31.8	9
Sweden	31.6	10
Norway	31.3	11
France	31.2	12
Canada	30.8	13
Austria	30.4	14
Germany	30.3	15
Iceland	30.3	15
Oman	25.5	17
Bahrain	24.8	18
Kuwait	24.8	18
Macedonia	24.1	20
Montenegro	23.1	21

The United States owns more guns per 100 residents, at 90, than any other nation in the world. The U.S. has over 50% more firearms per capita than the next two highest nations, Serbia and Yemen at about 0.55 and three times as many as major European countries such as France and Germany.

Source: Small Arms Survey

48. ☐ "Is it safe there"? ☐

[Homicide by firearm] In terms of raw numbers, column 1 is a ranking of countries with the highest total numbers of homicide by firearm (Brazil is highest). The second column shows the rate of homicide per 100,000 people (Honduras is highest). The third column shows total civilian gun ownership per 100 people (US is highest). Shown: top 20.

COUNTRY	Gun Deaths	COUNTRY	Deaths per 100,000	COUNTRY	Guns per 100
Brazil	34,678	Honduras	68.43	US	90.0
Colombia	12,539	El Salvado	39.9	Serbia	58.2
Mexico	11,309	Jamaica	39.4	Yemen	54.8
Venezuela	11,115	Venezuela	38.97	Switzerland	45.7
US	9,146	Guatemala	34.81	Finland	45.3
S Africa	8,319	St Kitts	32.44	Cyprus	36.1
Philippines	7.349	Trinidad	27.31	SaudArabia	35.0
Honduras	5,201	Colombia	27.09	Iraq	34.2
Guatemala	5,009	Belize	21.82	Uruguay	31.8
India	3,093	Puer Rico	18.3	Sweden	31.6
El Salvador	2,446	Brazil	18.1	Norway	31.3
Ecuador	1,790	S.Africa	17.03	France	31.2
Dom Repu	1,618	Dom Repu	16.3	Canada	30.8
Bangladesh	1,456	Panama	16.18	Austria	30.4
Argentina	1,198	Bahamas	15.37	Germany	30.3
Jamaica	1,080	Ecuador	12.73	Iceland	30.3
Vietnam	834	Guyana	11.46	Oman	25.5
Peru	757	Mexico	9.97	Bahrain	24.8
Puerto Rico	692	Philippines	8.93	Kuwait	24.8
Zimbabwe	598	Paraguay	7.35	Macedonia	24.1

Source: United Nations Office of Drugs & Crime

49. ☐ "Who's got the most people in prison?" ☐

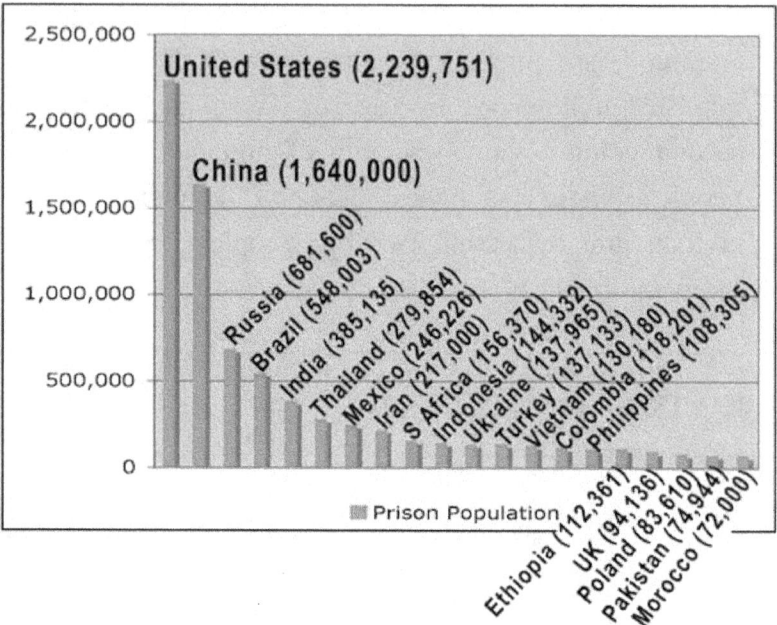

[Incarceration rates] More than 10.2 million people are held in penal institutions throughout the world, mostly as pre-trial detainees/remand prisoners or as sentenced prisoners. Almost half of these are in the United States (2.24m), Russia (0.68m) or China (1.64m sentenced prisoners). In addition at least 650,000 are reported to be in pre-trial or 'administrative' detention in China and 150,000 in North Korea (D.P.R.K.); if these were included the world total would be more than 11 million. The United States has the highest prison population rate in the world, 716 per 100,000 of the national population.

Source: World Prison Population List (10th Edition) Roy Walmsley, pub. International Centre for Prison Studies (ICPS) www.prisonstudies.org

50. ❏ "How's the health care there?" ❏

[Global health care] Here's how these 11 countries ranked overall in health care: 1. United Kingdom 2. Switzerland, 3. Sweden, 4. Australia, 5. Germany & Netherlands (tied), 7. New Zealand & Norway (tied), 9. France, 10. Canada, 11. US.

COUNTRY RANKINGS
Top 2*
Middle
Bottom 2*

	AUS	CAN	FRA	GER	NETH	NZ	KOR	SWE	SWIZ	UK	US
OVERALL RANKING (2013)	4	10	9	5	5	7	7	3	2	1	11
Quality Care	2	9	8	7	5	4	11	10	3	1	5
Effective Care	4	7	9	6	5	2	11	10	8	1	3
Safe Care	3	10	2	6	7	9	11	5	4	1	7
Coordinated Care	4	8	9	10	5	2	7	11	3	1	6
Patient-Centered Care	5	8	10	7	3	6	11	9	2	1	4
Access	8	9	11	2	4	7	6	4	2	1	9
Cost-Related Problem	9	5	10	4	8	6	3	1	7	1	11
Timeliness of Care	6	11	10	4	2	7	8	9	1	3	5
Efficiency	4	10	8	9	7	3	4	2	6	1	11
Equity	5	9	7	4	8	10	6	1	2	2	11
Healthy Lives	4	8	1	7	5	9	6	2	3	10	11
Health Expenditures/Capita, 2011**	$3,800	$4,522	$4,118	$4,495	$5,099	$3,182	$5,669	$3,925	$5,643	$3,405	$8,508

Countries were ranked on:
Quality: includes effective care, safe care, coordinated care, and patient-centered care.
Access: is there universal coverage?
Efficiency: national health expenditures and administrative costs and hassles, avoidable emergency room use, and duplicative medical testing.
Equity: Is it accessible across various income levels?
Healthy lives: mortality amenable to medical care, infant mortality, and healthy life expectancy.

Note: The most notable way the U.S. differs from other industrialized countries is the absence of universal health insurance coverage. Other nations ensure the accessibility of care through universal health systems and through better ties between patients and the physician practices that serve as their medical homes. June 2014

Source: Commonwealth Fund

51. ❑ "Do they have welfare there?" ❑

[Welfare states] Most every developed country in the world has welfare programs. It is based on the principles of equality of opportunity, equitable distribution of wealth, and public responsibility for those unable to avail themselves of the minimal provisions for a good life. The welfare state involves a transfer of funds from the state, to the services provided (e.g. healthcare, education) as well as directly to individuals ("benefits"). Here is how welfare programs have affected poverty in these countries.

Country	Absolute poverty rate (1960–1991)		Relative poverty rate (1970–1997)	
	Pre-welfare	Post-welfare	Pre-welfare	Post-welfare
Sweden	23.7	5.8	14.8	4.8
Norway	9.2	1.7	12.4	4.0
Netherlands	22.1	7.3	18.5	11.5
Finland	11.9	3.7	12.4	3.1
Denmark	26.4	5.9	17.4	4.8
Germany	15.2	4.3	9.7	5.1
Switzerland	12.5	3.8	10.9	9.1
Canada	22.5	6.5	17.1	11.9
France	36.1	9.8	21.8	6.1
Belgium	26.8	6.0	19.5	4.1
Australia	23.3	11.9	16.2	9.2
UK	16.8	8.7	16.4	8.2
US	21.0	11.7	17.2	15.1
Italy	30.7	14.3	19.7	9.1

Sources: Do Social Welfare Programs Reduce Poverty? Determinants of Relative Poverty in advanced capitalist democracies.

Religion

"It turned out I was pretty good in science. But again, because of the small budget, in science class we couldn't afford to do experiments in order to prove theories. We just believed everything. Actually, I think that class was called Religion. Religion class was always an easy class. All you had to do was suspend the logic and reasoning you were being taught in all the other classes."
— George Carlin, *Brain Droppings*

"I could prove God statistically. Take the human body alone - the chances that all the functions of an individual would just happen is a statistical monstrosity." - George Gallup

"When dealing with people, remember you are not dealing with creatures of logic, but with creatures bristling with prejudice and motivated by pride and vanity." — Dale Carnegie, *How to Win Friends and Influence People*

52. ❏ "How many Muslims are there?" ❏

[Religion stats] A Pew Research Center demographic study of more than 230 countries and territories finds 2.039 billion Christians (31% of the world's population; dropping), 1.6 billion Muslims (24%; growing), 1 billion Hindus (14%; stable), 775 million unaffiliated (12%; dropping), 300 million Buddhists (7%; stable;), 150 million atheists (2%), and 14 million Jews (0.2%) around the world as of 2010. More than 600 million (9%) practice African traditional religions, Chinese folk religions, Native American and Australian aboriginal religions. An estimated 167 million people—2.5% of the global population – belong to other religions, including the Baha'i faith, Jainism, Sikhism, Shintoism, Taoism, Tenrikyo, Wicca and Zoroastrianism, Rastafarianism, Scientology and others.

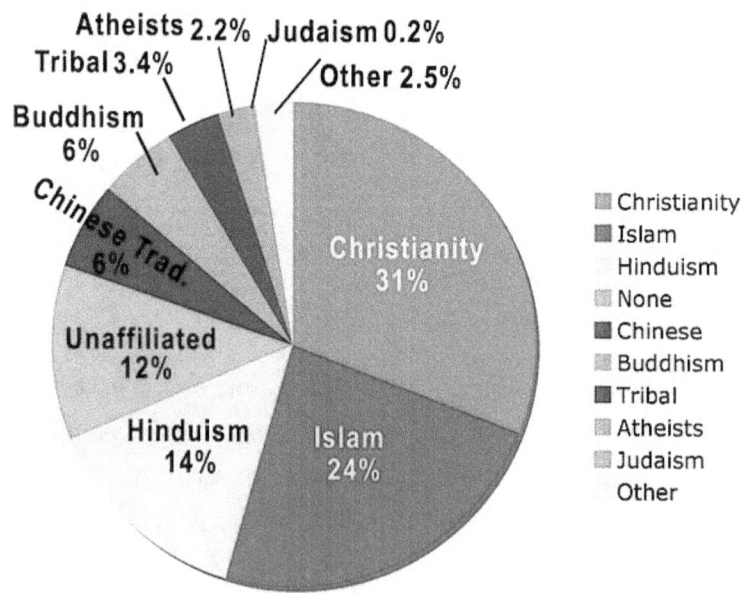

Source: Pew Research

53. ❑ "The truth about the Vatican!" ❑

[Vatican finances] Kept under of shroud of secrecy for centuries, the Catholic Church's financial, art, and real estate holdings remain a mystery. However, here are recently uncovered details:

Sex abuse settlements (approx. $1Million per victim) have cost the US Catholic Church approx. $1.3Billion.

The American church may account for as much as 60% of the Church's wealth.

Certain European real estate holdings (UK, Switzerland, Paris) purchased with money given to the church by Mussolini in 1929 in return for papal recognition of his fascist empire, is now worth over $843 Million USD.

In 2010, Italian authorities seized €23 million ($30 million) from a Vatican account at Italy's Credito Artigiano Spa, following allegations the Vatican's bank violated anti-money-laundering laws.

In 2012, the Vatican Bank and head, Ettore Tedeschi, were investigated on two occasions for money laundering.

JP Morgan Chase closed a Vatican account in Milan after the Vatican Bank was "unable to respond" to questionable money transfers.

Sources: The Guardian: How the Vatican built a secret property empire using Mussolini's millions
Forbes: The Vatican Bank-the most secret bank in the world
The Economist: The Catholic Church in America

A thought:
The predictable progression
of political pretense and
prevarication

Politicians have the luxury of lying with impunity at rallies, during interviews and at press conferences. With each new breaking scandal and subsequent statements issued, we've seen the same predictable sequence: (a) vehement denial, (b) claim of politically-motivated persecution, (c) initial admission to lesser charge, (d) tear-filled apology with spouse by the side, followed by (e) return to politics as usual once the furor subsides (think Clinton's Lewinsky, Christie's Bridgegate, Sanford's Appalachian trail). Unless forced to resign or unless faced with criminal prosecution, they know the public and media attention span and memory is short, and that another news story will always come along to displace theirs.

Well, what if, instead of once every two or four years, we conducted elections as "scandal specific" re-evaluations and recalls? In other words, what if immediately at the time of the latest scandal, a politician were required to conduct the first press conference connected to a lie detector, where his responses to media questions were evaluated, and at which his term in office would be immediately decided, on the spot, by the public who could vote him in or out via internet or smartphone? We just might shorten that predictable pattern of political pretense and prevarication. What do you think?

War

"There are no warlike people--just warlike leaders.
"—Ralph Bunche

"History is often made and buttressed by myths and
folklore rather than facts. — Daikichi Irokawa, *Age of*
Hirohito: In Search of Modern Japan

"War against a foreign country only happens
when the moneyed classes think they are going to
profit from it. "—George Orwell

"Great is the guilt of an unnecessary war. "—
John Adams

"Older men declare war, but it is the youth that
must fight and die. "—Herbert Hoover

"Until the philosophy which holds one race
superior and another inferior is finally and
permanently discredited and abandoned, there will be
war. "—Haile Selassie as quoted by Bob Marley in
"War"

54. ❏ "What's the long term cost of war?" ❏

[Post war suicides] There are many statistics that can be found of the expenditures, the casualties, the "cholateral damage" associated with war. One infrequently discussed statistic has to do with what happens to the men and women who fight these wars as they return home and attempt to assimilate back into civilian life.

Matthew Hoh is a Senior Fellow at the Center for International Policy and is the former Director of the Afghanistan Study Group, a network of foreign and public policy experts and professionals advocating for a change in US strategy in Afghanistan. A former State Department official, Matthew resigned in protest from his post in Afghanistan over US strategic policy and goals in Afghanistan in September 2009.

Here is a single statistic:

"...at least 22 veterans kill themselves every day. More than two of those veterans every day who kill themselves are Iraq or Afghanistan veterans...

...what that means for Iraq and Afghanistan veterans is that more veterans have killed themselves after coming home from Iraq or Afghanistan than have been killed in combat in Iraq or Afghanistan." — Matthew Hoh

Source: Democracy Now interview with Matthew Hoh. Nov 2014

Health & Survival

"Let food be thy medicine and medicine be thy food." — Hippocrates

"Healthy citizens are the greatest asset any country can have." — Winston S. Churchill

"I don't understand why asking people to eat a well-balanced vegetarian diet is considered drastic, while it is medically conservative to cut people open and put them on cholesterol lowering drugs for the rest of their lives." — Dean Ornish

"I never touch sugar, cheese, bread... I only like what I'm allowed to like. I'm beyond temptation. There is no weakness. When I see tons of food in the studio, for us and for everybody, for me it's as if this stuff was made out of plastic. The idea doesn't even enter my mind that a human being could put that into their mouth. I'm like the animals in the forest. They don't touch what they cannot eat." — Karl Lagerfeld

"Each patient carries his own doctor inside him." — Norman Cousins,

55. ❑ "This isn't the first ebola outbreak!" ❑

[Ebola outbreak history]

Mar 2014-Present	Multiple countries	Ebola virus	4655*	2431 (52%)*	Ongoing outbreak across multiple countries in W Africa.
Nov 2012-Jan 2013	Uganda	Sudan virus	6*	3* (50%)	Outbreak occurred in the Luwero District.
June-November 2012	Democ. Republic of Congo	Bundibu gyo virus	36*	13* (36.1%)	Outbreak occurred in DRC's Province Orientale.
June-October 2012	Uganda	Sudan virus	11*	4* (36.4%)	Outbreak occurred in the Kibaale District of Uganda.
May 2011	Uganda	Sudan virus	1	1 (100%)	The Ugandan Ministry of Health informed the public that a patient with suspected Ebola Hemorrhagic fever died on May 6, 2011 in the Luwero district,
December 2008-February 2009	Democ. Republic of Congo	Ebola virus	32	15 (47%)	Outbreak occurred in the Mweka and luebo health zones of the Province of Kasai Occidental.
November 2008	Philippine	Reston virus	6 (asymptomatic)	0	First known occurrence of Ebola-Reston in pigs. Six workers from the pig farm and slaughterhouse developed antibodies but did not become sick.
December 2007-January 2008	Uganda	Bundibu gyo virus	149	37 (25%)	Outbreak occurred in Bundibugyo District in western Uganda. First report of new strain.
2007	Democ. Republic of Congo	Ebola virus	264	187 (71%)	Outbreak occurred in Kasai Occidental Province. The outbreak was declared over November 20. Last confirmed case on October 4 and last death on October 10.
2004	Russia	Ebola virus	1	1 (100%)	Laboratory contamination.

2004	Sudan (South Sudan)	Sudan virus	17	7 (41%)	Outbreak occurred in Yambio county with measles in the same area, and several suspected cases were reclassified as measles
November-December 2003	Republic of Congo	Ebola virus	35	29 (83%)	Outbreak occured in Mbomo and Mbandza villages located in Mbomo distric, Cuvette Ouest Département.
December 2002-April 03	Republic of Congo	Ebola virus	143	128 (89%)	Outbreak occurred in the districts of Mbomo and Kéllé in Cuvette
October 2001-March 2002	Republic of Congo	Ebola virus	57	43 (75%)	Outbreak occurred over the border of Gabon and the Republic of the Congo. First time Ebola hemorr. fever reported in Congo.
Oct 2001-Mar 2002	Gabon	Ebola virus	65	53 (82%)	Outbreak occured over the border of Gabon and the Republic of the Congo.
2000-2001	Uganda	Sudan virus	425	224 (53%)	Occurred in Gulu, Masindi, and Mbarara districts of Uganda. using adequate protective measures.
1996	Russia	Ebola	1	1(100%	Laboratory contamination
1996	Philippines	Reston virus	0	0	Ebola-Reston virus was identified in a monkey facility in the Philippines. No human infections
1996	USA	Reston virus	0	0	Ebola-Reston virus was introduced into a quarantine facility in Texas by monkeys imported from the Philippines. No human infections were identified.
1996	South Africa	Ebola virus	2	1 (50%)	A medical professional traveled from Gabon to Johannesburg, after treating Ebola patient. He was hospitalized, his nurse became infected and died.
1996-1997 (July-	Gabon	Ebola virus	60	45 (74%)	Index case-patient was a hunter who lived in a forest camp.

January)					Disease was spread by close contact with infected persons. A dead chimpanzee found in forest at the time was determined infected.
1996 (January-April)	Gabon	Ebola virus	37	21 (57%)	Occured in Mayibout area. A chimpanzee found dead in the forest was eaten by people hunting for food.
1995	DemocraR epublic of Congo (Zaire)	Ebola virus	315	250 (81%)	Occured in Kikwit and surrounding area. Traced to index case-patient who worked in forest near city
1994	Côte d'Ivoire (Ivory Coast)	Taï Forest virus	1	0	Scientist became ill after conducting an autopsy on a wild chimpanzee in the Tai Forest. The patient was treated in Switzerland.
1994	Gabon	Ebola virus	52	31 (60%)	Occured in Mékouka and other gold-mining camps deep in the rain forest. Initially thought to be yellow fever; identified as Ebola fever in 1995.
1992	Italy	Reston virus	0	0	Ebola-Reston virus introduced into quarantine facilities in Sienna by monkeys from facility in the Philippines was involved in the episodes in the US. No humans infected.
1989-1990	Philippines	Reston virus	3 (asymp tomatic)	0	Three workers in primate animal facility developed antibodies did not get sick
1990	USA	Reston virus	4 (asymp tomatic)	0	Ebola-Reston virus was introduced once again into quarantine facilities in Virginia and Texas by monkeys from the Philippines. Four humans developed antibodies but did not get sick.

56. ❑ "Ebola is in the US!!! RUN!!!" ❑

[US Ebola deaths]

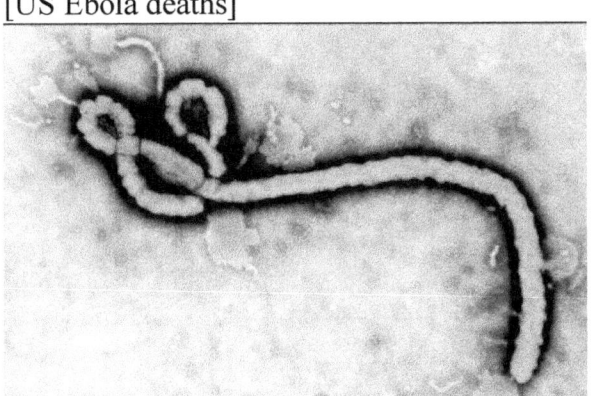

Fact: As of Nov 20, 2014, the number of people who have contracted Ebola *in the United States* who have died: **0**

Source: Public record

57. ❑ "Too much sun is bad for you!" ❑

[Health myths] Here are a few myths and counterintuitive "Believe it or not" health truths.

Myth: Milk does a body good. *Truth*: Cow's milk is essentially liquid meat in terms of its effect on the human body. It causes extreme acidity, which causes the bones to lose calcium in the body's attempts to balance the acidity. That's why countries with the highest milk consumption typically have the highest rates of osteoporosis.

Myth: Fluoride is good for you. *Truth:* Fluoride is a crude industrial waste product of the aluminum and fertilizer industries and is more toxic than lead, slightly less toxic than arsenic, and toxic enough to be used as rat poison.

Myth: Vaccines prevent disease. *Truth*: Since Gardasil's launch in 2006 until November 2012, the HPV vaccine was linked to 121 deaths and over 27,485 medical injuries of young girls, some as young as 11 years old. Other vaccines are linked to autism in children.

Myth: Sunlight is bad for you. *Truth*: Getting direct sunlight (no glass in between) for at least 30 minutes/day activates vitamin D production, kills bacteria on skin, improves mood, increases muscle strength, helps us absorb calcium, and improves the immune system.

Sources: The Fluoride Deception by Christopher Bryson
Silent Epidemic: The Untold Story of Vaccines (Gary Null)

58. ❑ "How to dodge a falling tree!" ❑

[Counterintuitive Health & Survival Tips] All other
things being equal, the
counterintuitive strategy for
avoiding being crushed by a
falling tree is to run *towards*
the tree rather than away
where the spread of the upper
branches will covers more area
(and you!) when it falls. We
live in a world where product
marketing has superceded
natural survival strategies that
now seem counterintuitive by
comparison!

Believe it or not: The best way to whiten teeth is to use
activated charcoal.

Believe it or not: The best way to cleanse the body is to use
dirt! Clay is a natural absorbent cleanses the skin, but taken
internally, cleanses the digestive tract as well.

Believe it or not: The best way to live longer is to eat less.
"Caloric restriction" gives the body rest in order to
rejuvenate and heal itself.

Believe it or not: The best way to stay healthy is to eat
lower down on the food chain (sprouts, grasses, single
celled algae, rather than the animals that eat them)

Believe it or not: Drinking sodas as way to quench thirst
has the opposite effect. Caffeine, and artificial sweeteners
like sucralose and aspartame, are diuretics which cause
dehydration which serve to increase thirst.

Sources: Fast & Grow Young by Herman Shelton
Yesterday's You: How to Reverse Aging, Livestrong.com

59. ❑ "You need chemo to treat cancer." ❑

[Cancer myth] This myth deserves a whole page, a whole chapter, a whole book devoted to it, and, in fact, many such have been written. Despite what you've been led to believe, the cure for cancer has already been found over 90 years ago, and hundreds who had been diagnosed as untreatable, incurable and given only months to live have been completely cured. Search on Youtube for "The Gerson Miracle" and "The Beautiful Truth" documentaries, and heed respected Dr. Joseph Mercola:

"Unfortunately, the leading cancer treatments in the United States are notoriously toxic and come with devastating, including lethal, side effects. Conventional medicine is so desperate to give the illusion of fighting the good fight that many of these drugs are used despite the fact that they're not really doing much to prolong or improve the quality of life of those diagnosed with cancer.

The best-selling (and extremely expensive) cancer drug Avastin, for example, was recently phased out as a treatment for metastatic breast cancer after studies concluded its benefits were outweighed by its dangerous side effects. Treating a disease that is in large part caused by toxins with toxins seems ignorant at best.

Cancer is, by and large, mostly a man-made disease, the tragic result of humans veering too far off course and avoiding health-sustaining diets and activities, while embracing a highly unnatural sedentary, stress-filled lifestyle with exposure to excess chemicals around every corner."—Dr. Mercola *Source: Dr. Mercola*

Sports & Entertainment

"3 out of 4 Americans make up 75% of the population."

"Death is 99 per cent fatal to laboratory rats."

'If there is a 50-50 chance that something can go wrong, then 9 times out of ten it will."

"It is proven that the celebration of birthdays is healthy. Statistics show that those people who celebrate the most birthdays become the oldest."

"I've missed more than 9000 shots in my career. I've lost almost 300 games. 26 times, I've been trusted to take the game winning shot and missed. I've failed over and over and over again in my life. And that is why I succeed."-- Michael Jordan

60. ☐ "Sports salaries are out of control!" ☐

[Pro sports salaries] Average annual salaries:

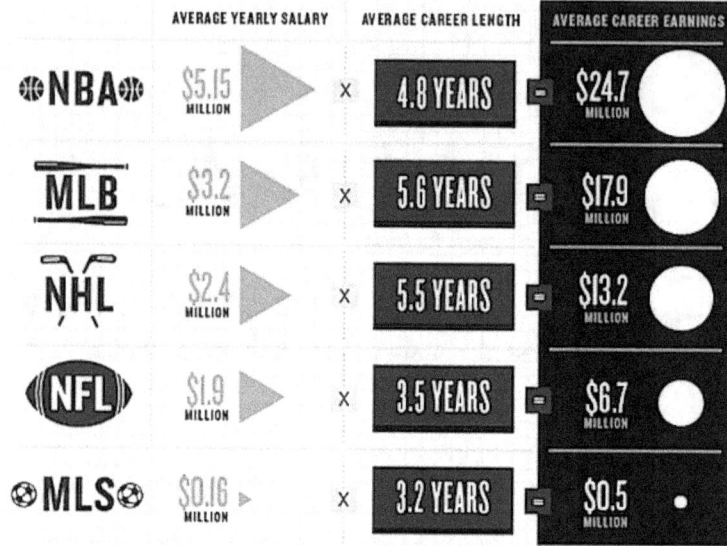

NBA (Basketball) players stand to earn the most

However, the "star" players earn considerably more:

And when you compute income based on scoring activity:

Alex (baseball): $253,968 per hit
Kobe (basketball): $37,940 per basket
Drew (football): $470,000 per passing touchdown
Sidney (hockey): $600,000 per goal
Thierry (soccer): $400,000 per goal. Source: USA Today

61. ❑ "And he can't even act that well!" ❑

[Movie industry] • Leonardo DiCaprio made $25M (incl bonuses) for "The Wolf of Wall Street," and $45M (est.) between June '13-Jun '14.

• Dwayne "The Rock" Johnson makes $15M per movie and earned $52million during the same time period

• Jennifer Lawrence earned $500,000 for the first and then $10million for the second "Hunger Games" movie.

• Liam Neeson earned $20M for "Taken 3."

• Crystal the monkey earned $108,000 in 2012 for appearing in nine episodes of NBC's Animal Practice.

Animation Director $200k	Hairstylist Trainee $66k
Art Director $134k	Lighting Tech (Entry) $53k
Assistant Art Director $101k	Location Manager $112k
Awards Show Producer $300k	Mechanic $59k
Best Boy $92k	Makeup Artist $100k
Body Double $33k	Model Builder $68k
Boom Mic Operator $87k	Music Mixer $111k
Chauffeur $56k	Noveliz Writer $12,500/book
Camera Operator $96k	Payroll Accountant $66k
Carpenter $61k	Personal Asst to Celeb $80k
Costume Dept. Super $91k	Projectionist (Studio) $72k
Costumer $79k	Prop Master $59k
Craft Svcs Foreperson $74k	Publicist (Studio) $93k
Dog Handler $54k	Scenic Artist $81k
Dialect Coach $125k	Script Supervisor $62k
Editor $95k	Sculptor $75k
Fire Safety Adviser $73k	Set Decorator $104k
First Assistant Director $192k	Sound Effects Editor $88k
Foley Artist $88k	Teacher (On-Set) $88k
Gaffer $59k	Trailer Editor $81k
Gardener (Studio) $50k	Wigmaker, Class 1 $59k
Grip $102k	Wigmaker, Class 2 $69k
Hairstylist $77k	Wild Animal Trainer $75k

Source: The Hollywood Reporter

62. ❑ "But, they don't make songs like before!" ❑

[Music industry statistics]   The total value of the recording industry in 2013 was 15 Billion.

51% came from physical format sales (cds, vinyl)

39% from digital sales (MP3 downloads)

7 % from performance rights (broadcast, internet, radio stations, venues, jukeboxes)

2 % from synchronization (use in TV adverts, films,)

The industry's digital revenues grew by 4.3 per cent in 2013 to US$5.9 billion.

Total investment in A&R (Artist & Repertoire) and marketing: $4.5 Billion

Over 28 million people paid for music subscription services in 2013. up 40% from 2012.

Japan is the 2nd largest market after the US

IFPI estimates that more than a quarter of Internet users worldwide (26%) regularly access unlicensed services.

Source: Intl Federation of the Phonographic Industry (IFPI)

63. ❑ "Beatles? Stones? Michael? Elvis?" ❑

[Best selling artist of all time] Okay, you know this argument is bound to come up sooner or later, so here are the numbers straight from Wikipedia, so you know they're legit!

Sales of 250 million plus units:

Artist	Origin	Period	Certified	Claimed*
Beatles	UK	1960-1970	certified units: 264.4 million	600 million
Elvis	US	1954-1977	certified units: 207.8 million	600 million 500 million
Michael Jackson	US	1964–2009	certified units: 174.3 million	400 million 350 million 300 million
Madonna	US	1979– present	certified units: 165.8 million	300 million 275 million
Elton John	UK	1964– present[	certified units: 161.6 million	300 million 250 million
Lez Zeppelin	UK	1968–1980	certified units: 138.5 million	300 million 200 million
Pink Floyd	UK	1965–1996	certified units: 114.6 million	250 million 200 million

200 million to 249 million records: Mariah Carey, Celine Dion, Whitney Houston, AC/DC. Queen, Rolling Stones, ABBA

120 million to 199 million records: Garth Brooks, Eagles, Rihanna, Eminem, U2, Billy Joel, Bruce Springsteen

100 million to 119 million records: Taylor Swift, Metallica, Britney Spears, Rod Stewart, Bon Jovi, Fleetwood Mac, George Strait

*Source: wikipedia; *claimed by other other media outlets*

A thought:
The fallacy of legality

Legality is not a defense for your actions. Neither should "illegality" be seen as an automatic prohibition. The term "legal" only has as much meaning as the society allows it to have. Remember, it was "legal" at one time to own other human beings. It was "illegal" at one time to marry someone of another race. It was "legal" and even an accepted form of family entertainment among whites in America to lynch blacks.

Legality is an idea, a construct of the people in power. Saying something is wrong or right simply because someone decided it was "legal" or "illegal" is a recipe for enslavement. Right-thinking people—those with a correctly functioning moral and ethical compass—should not be hindered by such constructs. It is necessary to think critically and come to decisions based on other determinants than mere "legality."

Sex

"Sex without love is a meaningless experience, but as far as meaningless experiences go its pretty damn good. "-- Woody Allen

"An intellectual is a person who's found one thing that's more interesting than sex. "-- Aldous Huxley

"Sex appeal is fifty percent what you've got and fifty percent what people think you've got. "-- Sophia Loren

"A liberated woman is one who has sex before marriage and a job after. "-- Gloria Steinem

"I haven't trusted polls since I read that 62% of women had affairs during their lunch hour. I've never met a woman in my life who would give up lunch for sex. "--Erma Bombeck

I remember the first time I had sex - I kept the receipt. " -- Groucho Marx

64. ☐ "Why don't you wait until marriage?" ☐

[Premarital sex] Here are some numbers from surveys of women and men aged 15-44 about premarital sex activity and opinions.

Percentage of men and women who had premarital intercourse:

Women (15-44 years of age) 86.4%

Men (20-44 years of age)   90.6%

"A young couple should not live together unless they are married."				
	Strongly Agree	Agree	Disagree	Strong disagree
Female	8.8%	22.0%	50.3%	18.0%
Male	8.0%	20.0%	55.9%	14.9%

"It is all right for unmarried 18 year olds to have sexual relations if they have strong affection for each other."				
	Strongly Agree	Agree	Disagree	Strong disagree
Female	6.4%	48.9%	28.7%	15.0%
Male	9.3%	52.9%	25.5%	11.2%

"It is all right for unmarried 16 year olds to have sexual relations if they have strong affection for each other."				
	Strongly Agree	Agree	Disagree	Strong disagree
Female	1.1%	13.7%	42.4%	41.9%
Male	2.2%	18.7%	43.6%	34.5%

"It is better to get married than go through life being single."				
	Strongly agree	Agree	Disagree	Strongly disagree
Female	14.7%	34.7%	36.7%	11.7%
Male	22.8%	43.2%	26.6%	5.4%

Source: CDC/National Center for Health Statistics

65. ❑ "Are you on the pill?" ❑

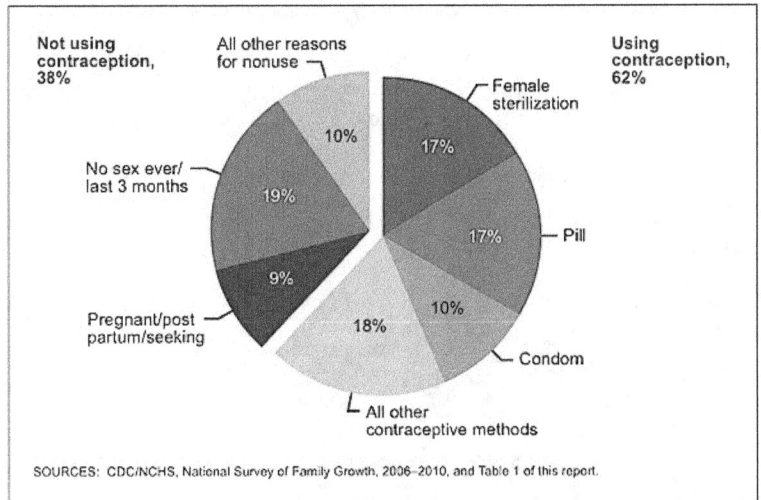

[Contraceptive use]According to the CDC, 62% of women aged 15-44 use some form of contraception. 38% do not.

By aged 40–44 years, 75% of women were using contraception.

The pill is more often used by younger women, whereas female or male sterilization is used more frequently by older women.

White women are more likely to use the pill (21%) as their current method of contraception than Asian (12%), Hispanic (12%), or black women (9.9%).

Source: Current Contraceptive Use in the United States, 2006–2010, and Changes in Patterns of Use Since 1995
by Jo Jones, Ph.D.; William Mosher, Ph.D.; and Kimberly Daniels, Ph.D., Division of Vital Statistics

66. ☐ "Of course I watch porn, but..." ☐

[Porn consumption] Those *against* porn *inflate* the numbers to show its widespread use and moral decay of society. Those who are *for* porn *deflate* the numbers because of the social stigma. Sex-negative societies tend to conflate prostitution, child molestation, trafficking, kink,  and porn into a single evil phenomenon. Therefore, it is difficult to generate accurate numbers for usage and revenues. With that said...*it's safe to say:*

"Porn usage is always greater than the statistics reveal."
Numbers (think: "it's probably more, but this is a start!")
40 million Americans visit porn sites regularly
Worldwide porn revenue (2006): 97 billion
US porn revenue (2006): 12.62 billion
Worldwide revenues of online porn: 4.9 billion
US revenues of online porn: 2.84 billion

Statistics for which accurate numbers exist:
• US Hardcore Pornography Titles Released:, 3200 titles (1994), 5700 titles (1995), 8000 titles (1996), 8000 titles (1997), 9200 titles (1998), 10300 titles (1999), 11500 titles (2000), 10900 titles (2001), 11700 titles (2002), 11400 titles (2003), 12000 titles (2004), 13588 titles (2005)
• 39 million homes receive adult channels. In 2003, Comcast, the largest US cable company, generated $50 million from adult programming.
• 50% of hotel guests order porn.
• 70% of hotel room services profits are from porn rental.
Source: A variety of sources courtesy of GrabStats.com

67. ❑ "Where is sex work legal?" ❑

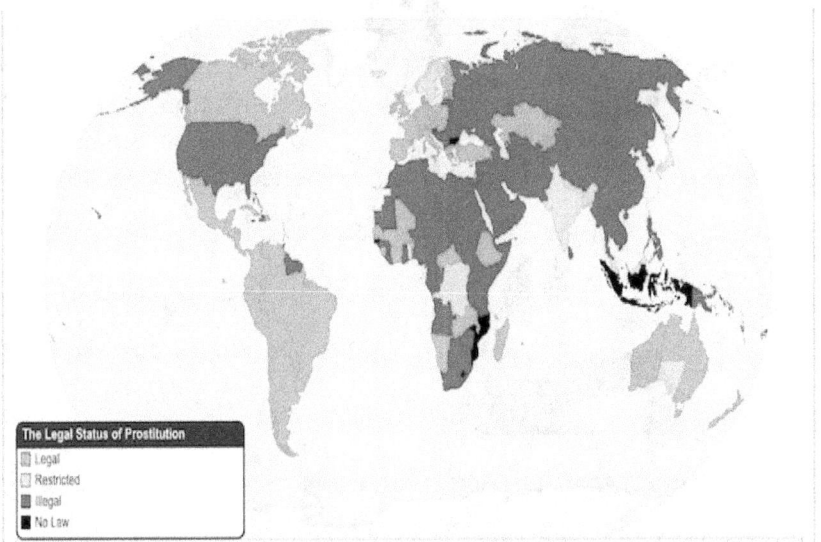

Countries where sex work is legal include but are not limited to: Argentina, Armenia, Australia*, Austria, Bangladesh*, Belgium, Belize, Bolivia, Brazil, Bulgaria*, Canada, Chile, Colombia, Costa Rica, Cyprus, Czech Republic, Denmark, Dominican Republic, Ecuador, El Salvador, Estonia, Ethiopia, Finland, France, Germany, Greece, Guatemala, Honduras, Hungary, Iceland*, India*, Indonesia, Ireland, Israel, Italy, Japan*, Kyrgyzstan, Latvia, Luxembourg, Malaysia*, Mexico, Netherlands, New Zealand, Nicaragua, Norway*, Panama, Paraguay, Peru, Poland, Portugal, Senegal, Singapore, Slovakia, Spain*, Sweden*, Switzerland, Turkey, United Kingdom(incl Scotland), US, Uruguay, Venezuela.

Limited Legality. The specifics vary by country and include things like where one can solicit, male vs. female prostitution (in Bangladesh, for example, female prostitution is legal while male prostitution is illegal. Sources: Sexwork.com, ProCon.org

The Legal Status of Prostitution by country ChartsBin

68. ❑ "He/she probably started at age 12!" ❑

[Sex work myths] The age of entry into prostitution is NOT 12 or 13 as is commonly cited, but closer to 16.* (US)

A recent study published by the New Zealand Ministry of Justice found:

Despite the perception that all sex workers are made to work by someone else, only 4.3% or approximately 28 of the 656 female participants in the study reported being made to work by someone. Sex work is a job some people have chosen and are happy doing.

When asked about the reasons why they stayed in the sex industry, the most common reasons were financial. Contrary to popular perception, only 16.7% reported working to support alcohol or drug usage, whereas 82.3% reported they needed the money to pay for household expenses. Sex workers enter the profession voluntarily for money.

Sex workers were more likely to be victims of crime rather than offenders.

Sources: New Zealand Ministry of Justice Report
* Is One of the Most-Cited Statistics About Sex Work Wrong?

69. ☐ "She looks like a porn star!" ☐

Do you fit the profile? From a study of 10,000 porn stars:
- Porn stars are 70% female and 30% male
- Men first get into porn at age 24; women 22
- Weight/Nat'l avg.: Men (167.5/194.7lbs);
- Weight/Nat'l avg.: Women 117/164.7lbs
- Avg height: Men 5'10"; Women 5'5"
- Average *f.* measurements: 34-24-34;
- Avg bra size: 34B
- Hair *f*: black (22.5%); brown (39.1%); blonde (32.7%); red (5.3%)
- Men stay in porn 4 years; women 3 years
- Where born (top 10): USA (2,850), Hungary (704), Czech Repub (536), UK (254), Russia (242), France (229), Canada (171), Germany (109), Italy (108), Brazil (88)
- Where from in US: CA(939); FL(216); TX(172); NY(148); OH(91); IL(79); AZ(78); MI(75); NV(74); PA(69)
- Tattooed: 24.4% of men; 42% of women porn stars
- Most common first names: Nikki, Jessica, Lisa, Kelly, Angel
- Most common last names: Lee, Love, Star, Fox, Rose
- Most common first names: David, Tony, John, Mike, Michael

- Most common last names: Lee, James, Taylor, Stone, Michaels
- Females often earn $600 to $1,000 per scene.
- Males earn less per scene $400, but have longer careers
- Porn star, Asia Carrera (10 yr career; 400+ films), dispelling the stereotype, is a member of MENSA International, the world's oldest IQ society, with an IQ of 156!

Sources:
Deep Inside: a study of 10,000 porn stars by Jon Millward
After Porn Ends Documentary

A thought:
PREDICTIONS

"That's what makes it relatively easy for some people to make 'predictions.' They simply know to be true what others still deny."

Remember when you laughed at those who said the government was taking away our freedoms? Now you have to relinquish bottles of liquid when you fly, and martial law is being declared willy-nilly.

Remember when you laughed at those who said that government has become "Big Brother?" Then, Edward Snowden revealed the NSA was spying on Americans and all of our emails and phone conversations are being collected.

Remember when you laughed at the "preppers" who pushed the need to stock up on survival products for when the fallout, plagues or epidemics came? Well, now ebola has people hiding out indoors for fear of being infected.

Remember when you laughed at the protesters who said the said the US was becoming a fascist police state? Now, you witness the militarization of the police forces, and tanks and tear gas being used on protesters in

Ferguson, Missouri in a response worse than that used by the Chinese government in Hong Kong.

Remember when you thought it despotic when Sadam used chemicals on his own citizens? Then, you watch the US police pepper spray US citizens—old and young—with impunity during peaceful "Occupy" protests.

Remember when you laughed at those who talked about government internment camps? Well, Texas governor Perry suggests those camps be readied for quarantining travelers suspected of having Ebola.

Predictions

For the most part, the realities behind what you've always thought of as "fringe" have always existed. Police have always been racially profiling. US monitoring of its civilian population was always true. It was happening even before Snowden revealed it to be so. The only thing that changed was public awareness of the truth. And so it is with much of what you now still consider fringe conspiracy thinking. Your unwillingness to accept the truth does nothing to change it. That's what makes it relatively easy for some people to make predictions. They simply know to be true what others still deny. They know to be true what others rely on mainstream media to validate. They know to be true what corporate interests obfuscate in order to generate money.

Therefore, it is with a certain degree of certainty that I can "predict" that:
- The vaccineophobes will be "proven" correct.
- Fluoride will be "proven" to be harmful.

- GMOs will be "proven" harmful, and
- Fracking will be "discovered" to cause earthquakes.

These are not predictions at all. The research and studies already exist. The evidence and proof is already there. All that needs to happen is for increasing numbers of people to become aware of what others already know to be true. That's how it's always been.

I cannot say precisely when these revelations will occur. I can only rely on the trends that are now more widespread to continue: Whistleblowers will come forward; investigative journalists will uncover truth; the guilty will confess to unburden their conscience or convict themselves by their own words; videos and social networks will reveal truth and reality to increasing numbers of people. Yes, the truth will out.

There is no need for me to make any predictions. If *you* continue to search for truth, rather than relying on others who are pulling numbers out of their asses, you can make your own.

Planet Earth

"Scientists were startled in 1980 by the discovery of a tremendous diversity of insects in tropical forests. In one study of just 19 trees in Panama, 80% of the 1,200 beetle species discovered were previously unknown to science... Surprisingly, scientists have a better understanding of how many stars there are in the galaxy than how many species there are on Earth."—World Wildlife Fund

"Scientific evidence for warming of the climate system is unequivocal." - Intergovernmental Panel on Climate Change

70. ❑ "I don't believe in global warming!" ❑

[Climate Change] We are beyond debate about the reality of climate change within the scientific community. The debate exists only in political and religious circles.

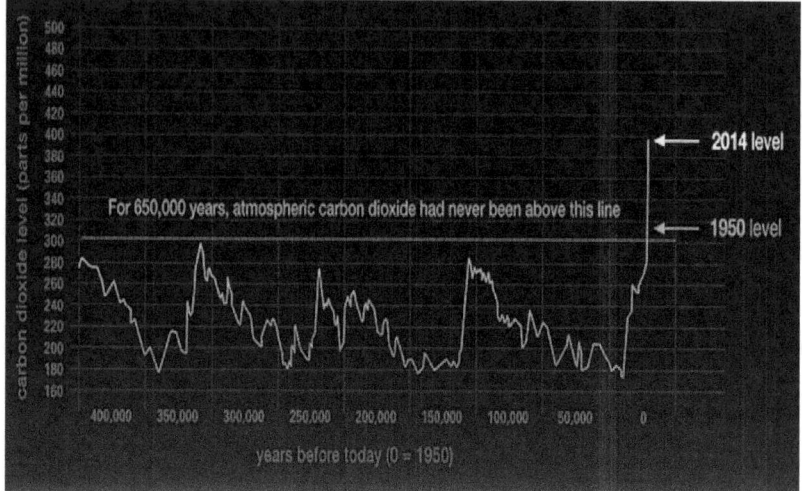

Carbon Dioxide levels: 398.5 parts per million and rising; the highest in 650,000 years.

Global temperature: up 1.4°F since 1880; nine of the ten warmest years on record have occurred since 2000.

Global sea level: up ~ 17cm. (6.7 in) in the last century

Warming ocean: top 700m (2,300ft) up 0.302°F since 1969

Ice sheet loss: **Greenland:**150 to 250 cubic km (36 to 60 cubic miles) of ice *per year* between 2002 and 2006; **Antarctica:**152 cubic km (36 cubic miles) 2002 to 2005.

Other evidence: rates and frequency of glacial retreat, extreme weather events, ocean acidification, decreased snow cover have all intensified over the past several years.

Source: NASA's "Global Climate Change Vital Signs of the Planet"

71. ☐ "Where did all the pandas go?" ☐

[Extinction Rates] The rapid loss of species we see today is estimated by experts to be between 1,000 and 10,000 times higher than the natural extinction rate.(a)

Experts calculate that between 0.01 and 0.1% of all species will become extinct each year. If the low estimate of the number of species is true—that there are 2 million different species on our planet (b)- then that means between 200 and 2,000 extinctions occur every year. If the upper estimate is true - that 100 million different species co-exist with us on earth- then between 10,000 and 100,000 species become extinct each year.

Class	Evaluated species	% at risk
Amphibians	6,300	33%
Birds	9,865	12%
Fish	8,814	21%
Invertebrates*	9,526	30%
Mammals**	5491	50% declining
Plants***	12,914	68%
Reptiles	2,828	21%

*1.3million known species of invertebrates, only 9526 evaluated
**1,131 mammals are endangered, threatened or vulnerable
***300,000 known plant species; 12,914 have been evaluated
(a)a.ka. the background extinction rate: the rate of extinctions that would occur if humans were not around.
(b) Between 1.4 and 1.8 million species have already been scientifically identified.
Source: *Center for Biological Diversity*

72. ❏ "Where's all the water going?" ❏

[Global water supply] Global freshwater demand is projected to exceed current supply by more than 40 per cent by 2030 at which time almost half of the world's population will be living in areas of high water stress.

97.5% of our planet's water is salt water, not freshwater.

Agriculture is the biggest water user, with irrigation accounting for 70% of global water withdrawals

Energy production accounts for 15% of the world's total water withdrawals (e.g. cooling power plants)

Approximately 15–18 billion m^3 of freshwater resources are contaminated by fossil fuel production every year.

At least 1.8 billion people world-wide are estimated to drink water that is faecally contaminated

Every day, 2 million tons of human wastes are disposed of in watercourses, and in developing countries 70 % of industrial wastes are dumped untreated into waters where they pollute the usable water supply

Part of the current pressure on water resources comes from increasing demands for animal feed. Meat production requires 8-10 times more water than cereal production.

Sources: United Nations Inter-Agency Mechanism
World Water Development Report

73. ❑ "Which countries pollute more?" ❑

["Ecological Footprint"] measures how much biologically productive land and water an individual, population or activity uses to produce the resources it consumes, and absorb the waste it generates (global hectares; farming, fishing, deforestation, carbon emissions.)

Two countries generated 31% of the world's total carbon Footprint: China (16%) and the US (15%). China is ranked 76th in per capita (individual) Footprint, but with the huge population has the planet's largest total Footprint. The *population* of the US is ¼ China's, but its Footprint is almost as large due to greater per capita consumption.

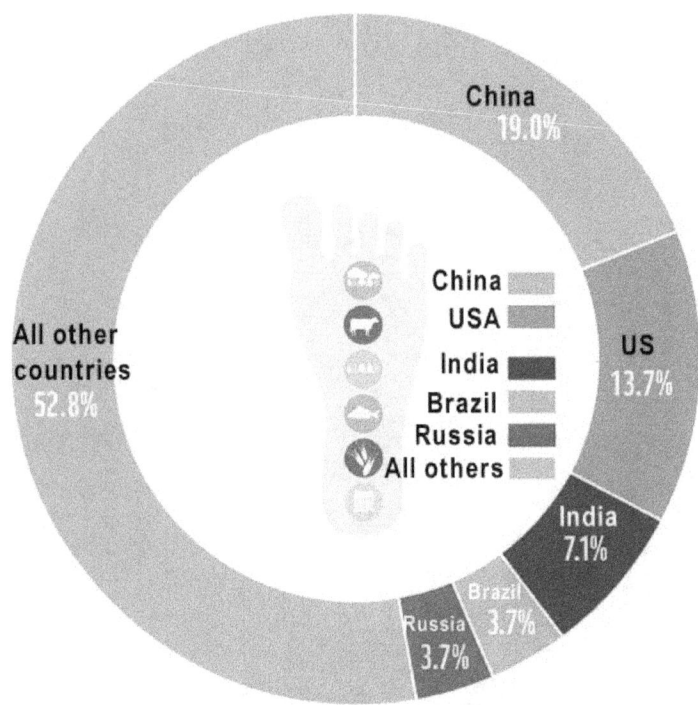

Source: World Wildlife Fund Living Planet Report 2014

74. ❑ "Where are the prime ecosystems?" ❑

[Biocapacity] "Biocapacity" is the ability of ecosystems to produce useful biological materials and to absorb waste (specifically, carbon dioxide) generated by humans. In other words, it is the ability of Earth to support the population. Almost 60% of the world's total biocapacity is located in 10 countries. For most countries, forestland represents the largest proportion of total biocapacity. Forests are particularly significant ecosystems because they provide services not only to local users, but also to others. As well as harboring great biodiversity, they play a significant role in climate stability through storing and sequestering carbon, and in the water cycle.

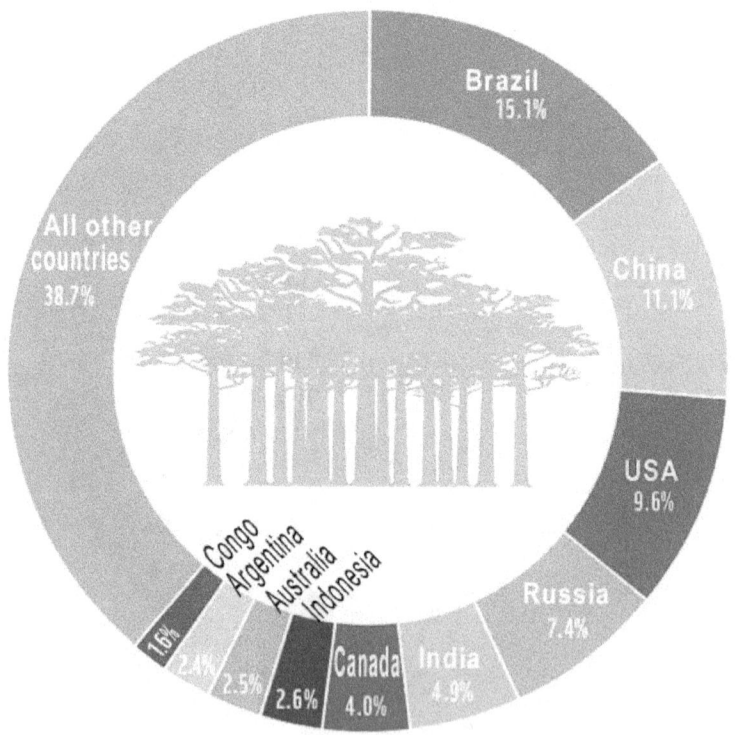

Source: World Wildlife Fund Living Planet Report 2014

75. ❏ "What is our planet's biggest crisis?" ❏

Planet earth's major global crisis in a simple graph:

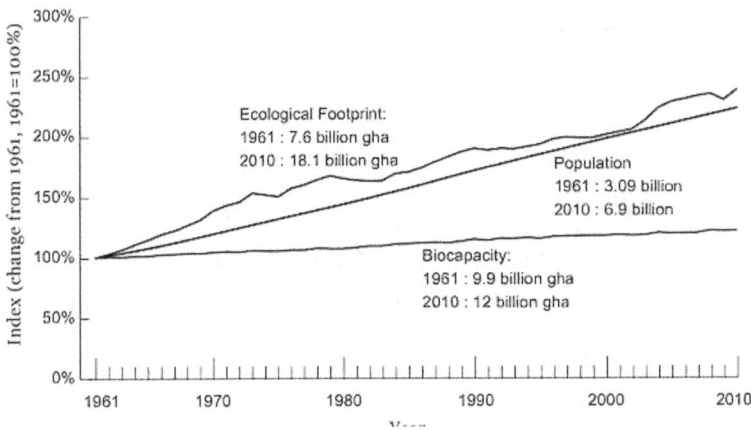

It's safe to say:

"As the earth's population steadily increases, the ecological footprint (our demand on the planet's resources) increases as well, but the biocapacity (what the planet can sustain) remains the same."

Source: World Wildlife Fund Living Planet Report 2014

A final thought:
WHAT YOU CAN DO
to change these numbers:

Many of the numbers in *Stop Pulling Numbers Out of Your Ass* represent conditions in our societies and throughout the planet that call out for change. The numbers for unjust incarcerations, Ebola outbreaks, air pollution, animal extinctions, global warming, etc., can change with your help. *We* donate a percentage of the profit of every sale of this book to the World Wildlife Fund. (See actual donation receipts at www.pullingnumbers.com). Here are a few things YOU can do:

☐ Volunteer

☐ Donate

☐ Join

☐ Vote

☐ Protest

☐ Write/Publish

☐ Share this book with others!

NEXT??
Tell us what topics you want to see!

Each section, and often each page of *Pulling Numbers Out of Your Ass* represents a topic about which an entire book of interesting facts, compelling insights and illustrative diagrams could be created. So, in the spirit of the *Chicken Soup for the Soul series*, what topic would YOU like to see covered in more detail and depth? Visit www.pullingnumbers.com/survey or email stop@pullingnumbers.com! Here are a few suggestions or make up one of your own!

Stop Pulling Numbers Out of Your Ass...about Planet Earth

Stop Pulling Numbers Out of Your Ass...about Immigration!

Stop Pulling Numbers Out of Your Ass...about Crime in the US!

Stop Pulling Numbers Out of Your Ass...about Sex!

How to Dodge a Falling Tree: More counterintuitive health & survival tips!

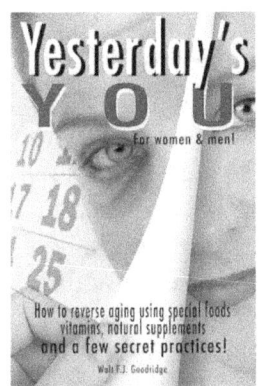

☐ Yesterday's You

How to reverse aging using special foods, vitamins, natural supplements and a few secret practices. Highly recommended as a companion to *Fit to Breed*

Paperback: $14.95;Ebook: $6.95
http://passionprofit.com/store/product.php?productid=116

☐ Fit to Breed...forever!

10 causes of impotence they don't want you to know about probably because there's no money in the simple cures that can help improve and mainting our erection. 150 truths, principles, causes, cautions, motivation, myths and facts plus a proven protocol of practices!

Paperback: $12.95;Ebook: $9.95
http://passionprofit.com/store/product.php?productid=117

☐ Fast & Grow Young!

Fasting is Nature's first cure. Fasting for extended periods leads to reversal and rejuvenation. Discover the secret.

Paperback: $16.95;Ebook: $2.95
http://passionprofit.com/store/product.php?productid=62

☐ **The Man Who Lived Forever**

The book that started it all, and upon which the Yesterday's You and Fit to Breed protocols are based. Read this "based in fact" story of perfect health, long life, and the fountain of youth, and discover the secrets to practical immortality!

Paperback: $14.95;Ebook: $9.95

http://passionprofit.com/store/product.php?productid=57

☐ **"If you want to be my girlfriend"**

a man's guide to setting standards, living and loving true to your self, getting and satisfying the women you want, all without every compromising your masculinity!

Paperback: $14.95;Ebook: $9.99

http://passionprofit.com/store/product.php?productid=114

☐ **Living True to Your Self**

Break free! Create the life of your dreams. Others have done it. Here are the thought processes that can make it happen for you, too!

Paperback: $14.95;Ebook: $6.95

http://passionprofit.com/store/product.php?productid=83

❏ About the author ❏

I.M. Sharp believes life should be lived with eyes open, with a willingness to embrace the counterintuitive and the determination not to pull numbers out of your own or somebody else's ass! Contact him via email at stop@pullingnumbers.com

"How to dodge a falling tree!"